Goa : A Lesson in L

CH00422065

By Adam Harkus

Back in August 2006 I visited Goa, India. A trip that affected my outlook on life, views on my country and my attitude towards others of all backgrounds. In 2015, I finally decided to put down in writing all the experiences encountered on my journey, not least my admiration for India, its people. its culture, and of course not forgetting its magnificent food! Its been a long time, some things have been forgotten, but hopefully you'll enjoy what's left.

adamharkus.com

Copyright © 2017 Adam Harkus

Contents

Chapter 1 : Mumbai

I'd arrived at the International Terminal of Mumbai Airport, waiting patiently at the baggage return for my guitar and suitcase. The suitcase appeared, but no guitar. Fantastic start. And so it began. First step; get the guitar back, and take it from there. The rep was super-polite as I rummaged through my documents in search of my destination address, Anjuna Palms resort, Anjuna, Goa. 'No problem' she said, "We'll send it on to you'. I didn't hold out much hope.

And so I found myself outside in the dark, amidst a manic crowd baying for attention, money, business, like a crowd of obsessed fans outside the backstage entrance after a rock concert. My only option was to hang a sharp left at the railing holding them back, towards what looked like some officially dressed guards. One of them engaged me, an older, thin, taller man with a calmness about him that stood out amongst the chaos. I needed to ask him how to get to the Domestic Terminal for my flight to Goa early the next morning, but he'd already pre-empted me. 'Domestic Terminal is closed, my friend.'

To this day, I still don't know if this was true or not. And so, in my own mind at least, the nightmare scenario began…

The guard had everything under control and planned out, the taxi was waiting, I'd have to stay in Mumbai tonight, according to him, no other option. As I felt the wheels of his plan turn in motion, I grasped at my other options, looking around for any other confused tourists in my predicament, but I was on my own, with no clue whatsoever. I hesitantly put my suitcase into the taxi and resigned myself to whatever happened next. Robbery? Kidnap? Murder?

The taxi pulled away from the airport and into the darkness, destination unknown. I hurriedly opened up discussions in the hope I could put my mind at rest, relieve the panic, at least know what was coming next. Predictably, his response was he needed money for the 'travel and 'hotel' expenses, I had none, so, first port of call:

cashpoint. I settled down in resignation, nothing I could do. A foreigner too far away from home.

After a dull journey through featureless, dark scenery, we eventually reached a small lit-up structure at the end of a deserted, almost derelict shopping precinct, nothing resembling a bank at all. I was ushered inside by the guard and the driver. Is this it for me? Not quite, as lo and behold, a cash-point machine sat in the back corner of the room, through some makeshift partitioning, along with, strangely, an attendant. The guard didn't ask for money, I took it upon myself to draw out £300 for some reason, but luckily and unexpectedly, I hit my limit of £250 for that day. Nothing anyone could do, If they were going to rob me, that's all the money that I had access to, for now. As we sped off towards the hotel my spirits lightened, I observed the hustle and bustle of the Mumbai suburbs, if that's where we were. Livestock roamed the streets and fires burned in the blackness, was it celebration or conflict ? Before I could decide the taxi come to a stop.

The hotel was palatial compared to what I had seen so far. I had a new theory, this was the scam: The domestic airport wasn't closed, they were simply getting some business for the hotel. Not the end of the world, then. As I emerged from the taxi a young porter boy appeared almost immediately to retrieve my suitcase. He was in traditional dress, a dark red tunic with white trousers and cap, in contrast to the official looking guard and driver. For the first time I could look the guard in the face without too much fear, and he ushered me towards the hotel staff, who, to my surprise, had arrived outside reception to greet me. The boy rushed through everyone and into the hotel with my suitcase as though his life depended on it, just as the guard introduced me to the staff who warmly greeted me.

Had I been over-reacting? Was I really in any danger ?

Inside the hotel I was immediately asked for my passport, and the tables turned again. The hotel manager tried to reason with me that it was standard procedure, but out of paranoia and something that I read somewhere about it being 'Illegal to give up your passport', I was back to square one again, I was definitely in trouble. So I became passive again and gave up the passport as the porter boy ushered me up to my room, leaving an uncomfortable atmosphere with the staff downstairs.

The hotel room itself was fabulous, all marble, brass, high ceilings and space, but to me, at this moment, merely a prison cell. I had no polite response to give the boy as he wished me a pleasant stay with the English he had took it open himself to learn, and as the door was closed I was completely alone, isolated, and lost.

Before I could settle there was a sharp knock at the door, it was the guard. I immediately went into attack mode, demanding answers, my passport, I had nothing to lose now. Why was I brought here? Was the airport really closed? How much was all this going to cost? How do I get back ? He put his hand on my shoulder and said something I will never forget.

'This is India my Friend'

He sat me down, told me to relax, everything had been arranged for me to make my flight tomorrow, and I could order anything I wanted. There was still the issue with my passport though, but he assured me it was just the norm, which I eventually accepted. Too tired to argue by this time. He produced some paper and a pen, as it was time to get down to brass tacks. Just how much was all this going to cost me? All my money ? would I need to go up to my limit at the cash-point again tomorrow?, will I even be allowed to leave?

After another heated discussion the end result was £30, all in. The same as a month's accommodation I had booked in Anjuna Palms. Although this place was a different class, I'd still been stung hadn't I? At least I now knew the damage. The guard, in his relaxed, efficient manner ran through the short itinerary; Order some food, get some rest, and he'd pick me up to get back to the airport tomorrow. I ordered a curry and beer, and the guard sped off down the stairs again. closing the door behind him. Would he live up to his word?

Before I had a chance to sort through my clothes for my stay, there was another knock at the door. It was the porter boy with the most delicious meal I had ever smelled, the mysterious spices immediately filling the room. And to go with it, a large chilled bottle of Kingfisher lager. This time I both acknowledged and thanked the boy, who seemed genuinely happy I'd given him my approval this time, and I settled down to what I'd hoped would be a taste of home, but the heat and spice of the Marsala was much more concentrated and vibrant, this was the real deal, layer upon layer of contrasting and complementary flavours and textures that made your lips sing, but none of the obnoxious heat of a hot curry back home, my very first real taste of India, with a cool refreshing lager to wash it all down.

Feeling a lot more relaxed and chirpier in general, I decided to run a bath. I noticed the time had ticked over to midnight, so six hours before my wake up call. I couldn't risk sleep of course, I needed to catch that plane, so I killed some of the time soaking in the bath, which was so huge I could lay flat in it. I observed my surroundings. The marble, the brass fittings, the stone floor. This was nice, at least £200 a night back home, so did I really have a lot to complain about at £30? Has anyone threatened me? No, Lied to me? I didn't know. Regardless, I'd been treated like a king so far, so maybe it was my own hidden away prejudices that had came to the fore. Then there was the other side, what if the domestic airport was open? what if I'm being charged over the odds for this hotel I shouldn't even be in? Why do they refuse to give me back my passport? I kept telling myself what the guard had said. 'This is India'. Maybe I wasn't as open-minded or tolerant as I thought I was, and this was my first culture shock. I finally made it out of the bath, got dressed and sat awake watching the minutes tick by. Whatever the truth of the matter was I was done with this hotel, I needed to be on my way. I'd exhausted myself by second guessing and over-analysing.

As the clock neared six am. my mood shifted again. This is it. Of course the guard isn't going to arrive and take me back the airport, and I'll never get out of here alive. I was drunk with tiredness at this point, but the adrenaline was pumping. Right on the dot of six there were two thudding knocks on the door that I recognised immediately as the guard's. True to his word he stood in the doorway, eager to get me moving, and I was only too willing to oblige as I gave the room a last glance, wishing It had of been a more comfortable stay.

Reception was a hive of smoky activity, much like the night before. The guard ushered me over to the the manager, an overweight, balding family man, who Immediately returned my passport, again, true to his word. His slightly stressed demeanour brought home the feeling that I'd been over-reacting, as I settled up the bill and attempted a clumsy and far too late apology. Nevertheless, despite everything, and even after they had my money, I was still treated with with the utmost courtesy, as the porter boy appeared again to take my case to the waiting taxi.

And so, just like the night before, I found myself outside the hotel. It was still dark, and the staff had once again gathered outside reception to see me off. Maybe this was all just part of the ruse, but I put that to one side for now as I shook the manager's hand and waved to the rest of the staff. The porter had completed his final task and my case was in the boot of the taxi, we were ready to go. But the boy and the staff lingered. The appreciation in the boy's face as I tipped him a few rupees still stays with me, as does the vision of the staff still waiting outside as the taxi sped off.

The journey back to the airport was silent. For me, too embarrassed, ashamed even, of my mistrusting, prejudiced, closed minded behaviour in my first night in Asia. For the guard, perhaps he'd had enough, and just wanted me out of his hands. As the scenery flew past I recollected the night's events without taking anything in.

Mumbai Airport: Domestic Terminal. The taxi ground to a halt by a dusty track outside the departures entrance. I now stood near the boot of the taxi with the driver and the guard as I experienced my first morning Indian sun beating down on my forehead, making my eyes squint. This was the part where I was supposed to tip the guard and the driver, but looking at the bustling airport made me question everything again. Of course it wasn't closed last night, why would it be? No tip. £30 was all they were getting out of me. I'd reached my destination. I was safe and back in control again. As I shook the guard's hand and bid him farewell he looked at me like a teacher looks at a student, maybe he understood my behaviour but in the end couldn't get his message through, so he just put his hand on my shoulder again and repeated his advice… 'This is India, my Friend'. And with that, he was on his way, back to the International terminal for his next fare no doubt. I quickly passed through departures and at last found myself sat on the plane to Goa, stepping through the events of the last twelve hours. This had been my first taste of India, who knows what surprises await in Goa. As the plane sped down the tarmac and into the air I sat back and finally got some rest.

Chapter 2 : Arrival in Goa

I'd read that Goa was the holiday destination of choice for the Indian people. A green. fertile land with idyllic sandy beaches. A party-goer's paradise. Maybe so. But this was off-season, a month too early, so I had no idea of what to expect. The plane cabin was just about empty, not a good sign, but the immaculate cabin crew still went about their business with the utmost professionalism and courtesy, something I'd become accustomed to throughout my trip. As we broke through the clouds to reveal the landscape below, my first thoughts were of the endless farmland landscapes back home, like a chequered quilt of greens, yellows and browns. As we stooped lower I noticed old hangars and aircraft that wouldn't have been out of place in an old war film, and as we touched down I tried to rid myself of any preconceptions I had. I didn't want another re-run of Mumbai. This time I was ready.

Goa Airport was unexpectedly modern and devoid of the EU rules, queuing and frustrations I'd gotten used to. Before I'd had a chance to have a look around the place I saw a short, grey haired, stocky man holding up a card with my name on it. This was Felix, the manager of Anjuna Palms. He greeted me like an old friend, although the only communication we'd had was via email a few weeks ago. I noticed the standard attire of the average Indian man to be a long sleeved shirt and trousers which seems a strange choice, given the heat, but I parked that thought for now as Felix took my suitcase and ushered me outside.

MONSOON. No sooner had we stepped outside but we were met with the most ferocious downpour of rain I'd ever seen. Water crashed into the pavement and onto the taxis across the road. Waves formed immediately creating a lake which powered its way down the hill towards the motorway. Nobody moved. This wasn't the type of rain to be walking in. This caused damage. The gaggle of travellers, business people and locals had various expressions. The excitement of the travellers at this act of God, the annoyance of the business people trying to get to a meetings and the (what would become familiar) shrugging of the shoulders by the locals.

And in a flash, blazing sunshine again and my first smell of the Goan air, fresh with delicious spices, but almost too dense to inhale at first. "Welcome to Goa" said Felix, with a knowing humour. I towered over him but felt like a child in his company. Just like a Mafia Don, he was the boss, head of his family and business, and my tour guide. And so we set off towards Anjuna. The bright, modern roadside billboards were all in English, promoting the affluent lifestyle of the west, all against a backdrop of hard manual farmland labour, where women of all ages tended to the crops in their vibrant, colourful garments. Just this vision made a big impact on me. Why the apparent love affair with the west ? The signs, to me at least reminded me more of propaganda than a simple commercial. All I could muster at this time was to ask Felix why everything was in English, to which he gave the rather brilliant answer "It's much easier to learn than Hindi my friend". With that I just sat back and enjoyed the beautiful scenery, the rolling hills, teeming with life and vegetation. This indeed was a happy, calming place. A welcome break from the rat-race back home.

We eventually stopped in a suburban area just outside Anjuna. Felix, without much of word stormed off into a nearby house. "I have to drop something off". So, with little choice I just sat back and waited, and waited some more. Thoughts went back for a moment to Mumbai, but fell away quickly as Goa was nothing like Mumbai, and Felix was nothing like the guard. I suppose I immediately trusted him despite everything. I needed to get used to the 'Indian' way of doing things. Don't question, don't rush, don't stress, be happy. After an inordinate amount of time, for back home at least, Felix re-appeared and we were on our way again.

Anjuna. I curiously tried to take everything in as we sped down the main strip and onto the hostel. The road was at least tarmacked, but no other structure even closely resembled home. Ramshackle huts that barely stood passed off as shops, cafe's and bars. There was no technology, no conveniences I'd become accustomed to. In a word, there was nothing and hardly anyone here. As we turned the corner I noticed a group of unsavoury looking locals gathered outside a bright blue hut on various motorbikes. I'd hoped Anjuna Palms would be nowhere near here, but alas, 50 meters or so up the road, we arrived at our destination.

The path to the hostel lead past the back of restaurant, which was also were Felix's livestock roamed and slept. After a month staying here, I still didn't get used to the combination of cooking oil and animal faeces in the air. His home was back down the path further still. A comfortable looking bungalow hidden away amongst some overgrowing trees. Felix's wife greeted me at the door with a beaming smile. She was taller than Felix with a dark perm and large round-rimmed glasses. If Felix was the manager, then his wife was the shop front. She immediately made me feel at home, even introducing their children who hid behind her, scared, like I was some sort of Alien. Felix said his goodbye's and sloped off, Leaving his wife to show me around.

The hostel itself was merely three separate one-bedroom rooms in a line, sharing a common terrace area with a kitchen/toilet/shower-room at the back. The padlocked wooden door looked like it could be pushed over by a small boy, and was constructed with ill fitting, partially rotten wood which left large gaps. But, at £30 a month, this was to be expected, even the insect colony on the ceiling didn't put me off. It was a room, with a bed, a table, a chair and nothing else. After Felix's wife finished up her 'tour' I immediately handed over the £30 up front. She wished me a pleasant stay and even offered to do my laundry, but I was impatient to get out there and explore asap.

I finally offloaded my bags, paperwork and personal effects. This was it. My first holiday alone. I could do what I want, when I want. My rules, my timetable. And so I set off down the path, past Felix's house, the back of the restaurant and right down to the gang of locals on the corner. "You want bike?", said an ancient looking man in the usual casual shirt and trousers. To which I shook my head, and noticed the collection of motorcycles and mopeds in the back of the 'shop'. Again, I'd been taught to never judge a book by its cover. This wasn't a crowd of vagrants, it was simply a motorcycle hire shop. "You want smoke?" They were all obviously spaced out on the local cannabis. To which I gave a polite "no thank you", pulling out my inhaler and humiliating myself by faking an asthma attack to demonstrate why I couldn't accept their kind offer. They all seemed to enjoy this, as the whole crowd came out of the woodwork laughing and joking amongst themselves. With perfect timing, I took another right and headed off down to the beach.

Anjuna is famed for its market, but as this was off-season, my immediate plan was to get to Calangute, the nightlife centre and the biggest town in the vicinity. But I had no map, no internet, I was going purely from memory and knew that Calangute (and its neighbour Baga), was the next town along the coast from Anjuna. Of course what I hadn't bargained on was the lack of road signs, or even roads for that matter, so I found myself at the edge of Anjuna, looking at a sign labelled 'Calangute' and pointing into the woods.

Amongst the humidity of the trees were mud paths that barely marked the surface. I found myself passing through tarpaulin and wooden structures, which back home would be no more than a children's den, but here were the home of entire families. This was real poverty. I had no right to be strolling through their home with my Next t-shirt and Primark shorts with handy over-sides pockets to fit my fat wallet. Yet the families seemed happy and content sleeping on the floor, with make-shift stoves made of rocks gathered from the nearby coastline. They waved and smiled as I fumbled my way in the undergrowth. I then reached a clearing, an overgrown graveyard as it turned out, and was soon met by a wall, then the cliff's edge. I turned around and couldn't make out the covered forest where I had been ten minutes earlier. I was completely, hopelessly lost.

Following my still 100% functional man compass, I came across what looked liked a tiny derelict church of some description. Outside was I can only describe as a tramp, a down-and- out, even in comparison to the families I had seen earlier. He obviously hadn't washed in weeks, was steaming drunk, had half of the undergrowth stored in his wild Jimi Hendrix hairdo and blood was pouring down his face. As soon as he saw me, he almost danced over, skipping over the undergrowth like a crazed chimpanzee. He grabbed my hands and started kissing them, refusing to let me go. "Calangute?" I asked, to which he glanced up, his eyes beaming "CALANGUTE!!!". he replied loudly, and pointed me excitedly in the direction. I thanked him and gave him a few rupees, to which he looked up at the skies, prayed to god and continued dancing by the derelict church in the undergrowth. I just about managed a smile whilst wondering for a moment how the man ended up in his situation.

True to the man's word I found myself on the path to Calangute. I picked up the pace, passing a small wooden kiosk, when I heard a voice "Hello my friend". A slight old grey man appeared from the kiosk, and beckoned me over. What now? Grudgingly I backtracked over to him. He stood there, motionless, seeming to look right through me, into my very soul. "Relax", he said with a smile. I looked down at myself, this clueless blunderbuss stomping through the woods, people's homes, upsetting the peace. To me I was fine, calm, relaxed, in control. But to the outside world and to this man in particular I was a quivering, stressed up train-wreck. From within the kiosk he conjured up a table and chair, as he opened up the front to reveal a bar. He then sat me down outside and served me a coke, the best kind straight from the fridge out of a glass bottle. I could feel the tension in my shoulders as I sat there, looking down the road to Calangute, my heavy heartbeat and laboured breathing. The old man continued to analyse me like a doctor, even coming over to massage the tension out of my shoulders before sending me on my way refreshed and relaxed.

Chapter 3 : The Road to Baga

As the old man disappeared into the distance never to be seen again, I passed a signpost pointing over a narrow babbling stream back to Anjuna, obviously the road I should have taken. This was the endpoint of the chaos and the beginning of my journey in earnest. As the dazzling sunlight ripped through dense trees either side of the path, the moistness of the previous rainfall was streamed away before my very eyes as the backdrop and atmosphere changed from forest to tropical. Locals passed with wide welcoming smiles and carefree abandon. I tried to adapt my regimented march into their rhythmic, relaxed stroll.

Although I'd lost track of time amidst the beauty of the path along the widening stream, It soon wound its way into a small village of wooden huts partially raised from the ground on small stilts, no doubt as a defense against flooding. I immediately noticed a barber's chair in the first, but they were all so similar, the others could have been selling anything, even just homes. I noted "lack of shop signs" in my virtual diary, but this area served people who would be classed as homeless back home. And yet there was no misery, no begging. This was a positive, happy place, quiet and relaxed, and I passed through almost unnoticed.

As I reached a junction the stream had now become a river, to my right was the path to Baga/Calangute, to my left was another way back to Anjuna and, to my surprise, a partly built apartment block. Skilled, gymnastic builders climbed the concrete and steel structure above an already completed salon and convenience store, no hard-hat, protective gear or even shoes here, this was manual labor with the most basic of tools. I looked back to the village just back up the path, my first experience of the contrast between old and new Goa right here. This was a place of rapid expansion and building work, seemingly oblivious, or worse, uncaring towards the traditional communities in the woods. Why would anyone need a salon here anyway? As I took the right turn to Baga, I noticed the answer. A large, sprawling holiday complex over the river, empty and out of season, I felt lucky to have avoided the crowds and continued down the path as the heavens opened once again.

The regular roadside pauses out of the rain broke up my progress, but with each passing moment I was shifting away from my default western mindset. I looked back on my journey from home, to Mumbai and even from the hostel. It had been an adventure I should have savored. It doesn't always have to be about getting from A to B in the shortest route or the fastest time. It should be about enjoying the journey. As I stood sheltered under a vast canopy of a giant tree, I stopped caring about how long this spell of rain lasted. Instead, I just took a breathe, admired the scenery, and moved along until the next spell, Baga was close now and I couldn't wait to see it.

Eventually the path twisted towards the widening river as an ugly, monolithic, concrete and steel bridge loomed into view. Typical of the 'modern' Indian buildings I'd seen so far, the workmanship consisted of still protruding steel rods and large square concrete blocks all clogged together with cement, probably in double quick time. I imagined the locals would say It served a purpose and got you across the river, so what's the problem? Nevertheless, the complete lack of architecture and design of this monstrosity against the beautiful backdrop always made me smile. Indian's have no hangups about this sort of thing at all. I broke into a half-sprint, the only way to get up enough momentum to make it up the almost vertical concrete ramp, which looked to be disintegrating under my feet, and with a final push eventually made it into an uncomfortably narrow tunnel. I kept up the pace out of a childish fear of the dark and enclosed spaces and eventually emerged in Baga.

As I looked back over the river I could see it expand into a small lake, and then out into the Indian Ocean. I could see the Baga coastline with its sandy beach and palm trees in the distance to my left and the impassable cliff face hiding the Anjuna coastline to my right. In the centre the glowing orange Indian sun casting its hazy magic over this perfect picture postcard. I stood for a moment as my breath was taken away, before realizing the monsoon had broken the river's banks so that my path to Baga beach was cut off.

Back in England I would have turned back. An unacceptable situation. What about my shoes? What's in the water? Would I drown? But here, no worries. I plodded through the marshes knee deep with my wallet in hand, out of the way. Back home we worry too much, paralyzed by the anxiety of trivial dangers, or even just change. I acknowledged the smiles of others, almost waist deep in the water compared to myself, and then the smiles turned to laughter. This was an act of God, and nothing anyone could do about it. With tired legs, a welcome sight. A public convenience. Similar to the bridge, another concrete monstrosity, gigantic in size but this time painted in a slapdash red and white striped colour scheme, just incase it didn't clash with the scenery enough. An eyesore, but at least now I was out of the water.

At last I crossed over the main road that passed through Baga and Calangute, and made it onto Baga beach, which was bustling with the Indian holidaymakers I'd heard about. Men, women and children of all ages, rejoicing, playing and laughing in complete abandon, free of any westernized notion of 'cool' or 'proper'. This was just families and friends letting their hair down. Women, modestly fully clothed, Fathers somersaulting into the sea and packs of children in their element. I imagined a similar scene at the coast back home, in its heyday, before the EU regulation and uncaring councils strangled the life out of everything. I stood back to observe them in the distance, being the outsider, but I was soon called over.

Like a long lost cousin, I was greeted by a couple of similar age with open arms and huge smiles. The cameras were out as they excitedly engaged in small-talk. My height was something of a revelation to them as I towered over them in my still wet-through clothes. This was common, as westerners were perceived as near movie stars over here, or rich, successful businessman / sports stars at least, something I wasn't altogether comfortable with given my lowly call center status at the time. More than that though, the people of India seemed unaware of their own considerably more human assets. Another picture for the scrapbook.

It was high time for a rest, so I happened open a 'Coffee Day' outlet at the side of the road to Calangute. As I ordered and sat down I again observed my surroundings. This place was another step towards the modern, tourist-centered Goa, Just opposite a branch of Subway, it was the most chrome and glass I'd seen so far. A young, spectacled lad ran the show single-handedly, as an army of customers and friends looked on in admiration. To him, he was on the first step to bigger things, to fulfilling his dreams, so he was going to be the best he could be, and all his friends were behind him. I'd never seen someone take such a pride in his work and position, but, as I was beginning to understand, this was another 'Lesson in Life', this was why Indians are the best waiters in the world, this is how they are able to come over to our country and build up a business from nothing. Indians are always looking to better themselves, for themselves and their family. Indians would never turn down a job in a cafe or a McDonald's because it was beneath them, unlike back home. Indians would never scrounge from the state, they don't have that option here.

As I pondered the shameless laziness of the British benefits culture, I saw another side to the lad, why the fascination with the west? What were we doing that was so right? Is it really all about money at the end of the day? What about traditional Indian history and values ? Those are questions I returned to throughout my trip, but nevertheless, for better or worse, Goa was changing, and all I could do for now was admire the lad just like everyone else in the cafe that day.

Chapter 4: Calangute

As I headed off down Baga-Calangute road, the heavens opened once again. I ran for shelter into what revealed itself to be an internet cafe, a popular site in Goa. It was a hive of activity, teams of friends were deeply engaged in a session of online-gaming, totally oblivious to their surroundings. I merely wanted to keep up to speed with the social-network activity back home, something I would rely on more and more as the days passed by. Technology wise, we were still in the 90's and I became hypnotized by the grindingly slow egg timers and progress bars which eventually loaded up comforting images and updates of home. As I looked outside at the scene of ramshackle shops, mopeds and thundering rain, it sank in just how far away home was.

Power cut! Being the only one in the place to registered any sort of reaction, I looked helplessly at the attendant. Just like the lad in the Cafe earlier, this young man was completely devoid of any western cynicism. This was his business and he ran it like clockwork with obvious pride. I took the opportunity to inform him that this was my first day in Goa, as if he cared, to which he responded in typical Indian style to just sit back and relax until the power came back on. I thought back to the old man at the kiosk in Anjuna, maybe I still hadn't got to grips with this pace of life yet. The rain had now stopped however, so I opted to carry on down the road.

The road to Calangute was lined with empty 'theme' bars, cafe's, hotels and shops off all descriptions and conditions. From chic modern looking bars with palm trees and open-air VIP lounge areas to run-down launderettes. A mish-mash of old and new Goa catering for it's traditional residents and holiday makers. The young student travelers and old hippies from abroad to the big-guns from the big smoke of Mumbai. A melting pot of cultures in total harmony and celebration.

This was still only day one though, so for now I just took note and carried on walking against the deafening backdrop of traffic horns and straining moped and car engines. This was the traffic etiquette of

India; use your horn to communicate a request for space, a demand to get past, a thank you. Like an ugly, mechanical bird song. But predictably there was no road rage, no conflict, despite the complete lack of rules or structure, just like most things in India, the system just worked, somehow.

Eventually I arrived at the center of Calangute. The all too familiar souvenir shops lined a path to my right, along with a few restaurants I knew I'd be sampling at some point. This wide central area felt like my ultimate destination and seemed to be a focal point of all activity, with taxis lining the curbs, driver's touting for business and the frenetic activity of a school finishing for the day. I'd been on the go since leaving England over 48 hours ago but a flight of stone stairs beckoned me onto the beach, which seemed much larger in scale to Baga, and was even more crowded.

A large restaurant stood to my left, its flimsy wooden structure seemingly propped up on stilts and vulnerable to the elements. Another time perhaps, as what grabbed my attention for the moment was a typical clumsy block of concrete away from the crowds, which, on closer inspection turned out to be bench, simply labelled 'Tourists'. Unhindered and unnoticed, I wearily made my way over the still burning sand and, at last, came to stop. As I watched the droves of holiday makers in solitude whilst occupying my very own throne, the need for a 'new Goa' dawned on me, with all the tourism and prosperity it would bring. Tourists were respected here, a little too much for me to be comfortable with. I didn't need my own bench, I wasn't better than anyone else, so I moved over to the centre of the beach, amongst the crowds, and completed my protest by clumsily slumping to the ground like a tired elephant.

I gazed out into the Indian Ocean, wondering which direction home was over the horizon. How many miles away and what time of day. The crashing waves and sounds of celebration were almost tuned out by the still calmness of the almost setting sun and the intoxicating flavours of the east passing in the breeze. I was like an island, alone in my thoughts, but then the calm was broken by a rumble of thunder. I stayed put for the main event, as did everyone else, as the warm orange pastel of the horizon was engulfed in almost total cold blackness. A swirling, violent, elemental backdrop on the canvas of paradise. Looking back to the steps, the match-stick wooden structures looked to stand no chance, and as the sun was almost filtered out completely, the rains came, like daggers on my brow, peppering the tarpaulin roofs of the beach shacks into submission. Time had stood still, as if the whole of Calangute was holding its breath, and then the breathe was let out as the backdrop shifted again as quickly as before, but this time the sun was even lower, as though time had sped up during the darkness.

It was time to leave, time to eat. I was swept away amongst the crowds as they gathered up their belongings and huddled back up the steps. What would my very first meal in Goa be? The restaurants, all advertised in English, were mostly vegetarian, with only a few labelled 'non-veg', or in the other words, the opposite to back home. I was drawn to a large building back at the crossroads of the Baga/Calangute road, so in I went, up a flight of stairs and into a completely empty restaurant with immaculately laid tables. An old grey man greeted me, seemingly dressed in the same garb as the porter boy back in Mumbai, and proudly welcomed me inside, like it was his own home. This was the way in India, no matter where you were, a restaurant, cafe, bar, hotel. The staff made you feel welcome, they made you smile, they made sure you were happy. Back home, we had disgruntled staff on the minimum wage, bitter about having to work such a lowly job. Here, they had pride in their work.

I had no interest in looking through the vegetarian menu, rather I wanted the waiter's recommendation, to which he raised his finger in acknowledgment with a grin, spinning on his heels and straight back through the door to the kitchen. I sat overlooking the main road i'd walked the length of earlier. Droves of local noisy twenty something's on mopeds passed by, the atmosphere building to maybe some sort of event later in the evening. For now though, a large bottle of Kingfisher had arrived at my table, which the waiter opened and poured into my glass. I'd never heard of the brand before, but it was everywhere here, emblazoned on billboards, hotels, restaurants, bars, and even planes. It was the archetypal easy going 4%-5% larger. Its simple, cool crispness the ideal accompaniment to the complex, multi-layered fireworks that is Indian food.

And so the best meal I've ever eaten was presented to me. A vegetarian Thali, or an assortment of dishes, each in their own small metal bowl, placed in a circle around a central helping of naan. As my senses were assaulted from all angles with the wildly varying heat, textures, flavors and aromas, not a single dish was recognizable from back home. One I could've sworn was chicken, but may have been tofu or something similar, some, like the best Bombay and Sag Aloo I'd ever eaten, or a simple marriage of red onion and lemon juice, or a weird and wonderfully tangy-sour cheese dish played accompanying roles, while others, including a variant on 'Butter Chicken' demanded my full attention, with its addictive, thick, moreish gravy seeming to be a perfect match for my taste buds and combining the sweetness of a korma with the cutting heat of a madras and all points of texture and spice in-between.

Although I was given a knife and fork, here, you ate with your hands. So I hungrily went about the task of tearing off a piece of Naan, and using it to dip, shovel and grab from the smorgasbord of dishes, washing it down with the cool larger. From time to time the cheery waiter would top me up, almost unprompted, expertly avoiding to distract or bother me in any way, whilst still being constantly on hand if needed, the consummate professional. Rice was strangely absent. but I would soon be introduced to proper Indian Biryani later. That's another story.

As the last few morsels were finished off, I slouched back into the chair, 100% content with life. As the waiter gave me a knowing glance I could only look at him wide-eyed as I released a sigh of overwhelming satisfaction and signalled for the bill. If memory serves me right, I looked down the list of items I'd ordered, which came to a grand total of just over £1 English sterling. I doubled it, as anything more may have been deemed an insult and thanked the waiter for a level of food and service I'd never experienced before, and never would again outside of India.

I made my way up to a taxi rank around the corner, as Calangute was nearing its night-time shift. I noticed a 24 hour complex of bars and shops I'd return to another day, but for now it was home-time for my tired legs and full stomach. The Cadillac style taxi felt like a waterbed as I reclined to almost horizontal in the back and simply called out the request 'Anjuna Palms'. I noticed the moustachioed driver was wearing what looked like a sea captain's hat as I began to drift off, trying to pick out my location as neon lights whizzed past in the darkness. I was soon snapped out of it as the driver screeched to a halt outside the bike shop on the corner I'd passed earlier that day, The attendants still stood outside, conversing and smoking, in fact, I don't even think they'd moved a muscle since I'd been to Calangute and back.

After paying the taxi driver I found myself back in my room. It had been an exhausting but exhilarating day, but before I had a chance to rest, there was a knock at the door, Felix's wife. "We have a delivery for you". I followed her through to the house where a young lad had just arrived on his moped, obviously a bit worse for wear after a long journey. He untied a large oblong package which was strapped to the frame and handed it to me with the hope of a tip in his eyes.

My guitar had arrived.

Chapter 5: Mapusa

Dawn of my first morning in Anjuna. I'd slept soundly and for the first time felt refreshed, relaxed and together. I looked down at the guitar case at my bedside and remembered my purpose for being here. The plan, as crazy as it seems looking back, was to earn some money busking, and crazier still, teach some karate. The pipe-dream seemed distant now though, as In my short time in Goa I'd not seen any live music or other buskers, nor anything even approaching martial arts of any sort. But that was the westerner talking back then, the man with the plan, and after only 48 hours in India I was softening, my breath slowing. So I parked the plan, instead waiting to see what presented itself rather than bulldoze my way through the woods like yesterday.

Instead I decided to jump on a bus, I'd seen 'Mapusa' appear on many of the road-signs, so figured it was some sort of traffic hub, perhaps a large town or city. I gathered myself and crossed the road outside Anjuna Palms, noticing a cafe/bar establishment. Out of curiosity I wandered over. Like quite a few establishments nearby, this had a trendy, hippy vibe to it, with a bright interior of hand painted imagery and national flags, almost Jamaican in style. Long benches were situated throughout to accommodate the passing travelers and party-goers, but at the moment, off-season, everything was eerily empty and quiet. I noticed also an adjoining internet cafe, very handy, but I could see some activity outside, the bus was on its way.

I'd thought Mapusa was pronounced 'Ma-poo-sa', but as the ancient coach flew past, a dexterous young man lurched out of the window, 'Mapsa', 'Mapsa'. To which the gathering crowd acknowledged him as the driver slammed on the brakes covering us in a plume of dust. I noticed the bus was covered in ornamentation and brightly, intricately painted. Despite its obviously poor condition, there was a lot of love spent on it. The interior cranked up the ornamentation even further, with religious, joyous daubing and over the top chintz, even the odd miniature statuette. Goans had a strong, mostly Christian faith, which was evident all around.

Another thing about Goa, and maybe India in general was the social position of men and women. As I entered the cramped coach, the women, regardless of age, gave their seats up for the men. At first I refused, but the women seemed all too happy with the situation, so rather than risk insulting them, I squeezed my frame into the child-sized seats, red-faced, and acknowledged their kind gesture. The driver/assistant double act really was something else, harking back to the golden days of 2-man driver/ticket inspector buses back home, but this was true Indian style, with the agile, 'inspector' (for want of a better word, although that hardly does him justice) hanging out of the bus at regular intervals, like a racing side-car passenger, calling out the destination of 'Map-sa' to any unsuspecting wandering locals, as the driver turned on a sixpence through the ever more winding roads and narrow dust-paths. The coach seemed ready to disintegrate, but we had the Lord Jesus covering our backs, or so it would seem. As we sped towards our destination, the coach became ever more crowded, until we were packed in like sardines. No stress-heads here though, in fact the main concern in people's faces was how comfortable the visiting westerner was, with the lack of legroom pushing up my knees to almost chest height.

Occasionally, we would come to an abrupt halt. Cows, as it turned out, were highly respected, revered even, probably for religious reasons. In any case, they were free to roam, unchecked, wherever they liked, even on busy roads. The incessant sounding of horns all died down as a herd of cattle slowly trundled by, as though we were in the presence of royalty. I looked on, with my now familiar bemused expression.

My first impressions of Mapusa weren't great, it was an exceptionally drab looked town, maybe even soviet-looking in nature, but also reminding me of the regular images of middle-east war-zones on the news back home. A dour, commercial district of ugly concrete without any outstanding architecture of note. To sum up: Completely depressing. As the packed-in passengers eventually squeezed their way out of our ridiculously decorated ride, a wall of heat smashed me square in the face, almost flooring me there and then. As I gathered myself i noticed we were in an outdoor coach terminus, with each individual coach personalized with its own unique branding, like a classic coach show of some description. Looking over to the Terminus building itself, I was shocked to see what looked like dead bodies, both animal and human, just laying on the ground, on closer inspection though, it turned out this was just the way to deal with the intense heat, like a family dog on a hot day at the park, but the imagery of the apparent dead bodies against the depressed, grey backdrop left a lasting impression on me, as though I was seeing the aftermath of a nuclear attack.

With no plan or direction, I attempted to merge in with crowds, which were all moving towards a long, ominous looking wall at the other end of the terminus. An opening appeared, and I found myself, uncomfortably, in the midst of a hectic, feverish local market. My senses were assaulted from all angles, the horrendous overcrowding, the noise of shouting and haggling, the fragrant spices and the sweltering heat. I was soon being shoved along, almost with the droves of frenzied bodies under my feet. I stopped and stood firm, letting the crowds disperse around me, to admire the spectacle of the occasion. Fruit of all descriptions and vivid color, stacked high, and even encroaching well into the thoroughfare, the intense aroma of spice stalls, unusual pastries of all shapes and sizes, too many even to ponder. I quickly lost my bearings as I was engulfed in the crowds like swarming ants, until a friendly face caught my eye by a clothes stall. The young boy sliced through the crowds towards me and somehow, expertly, created some space in front of us, ushering me over towards a central pavilion-type area.

"You want food?" he said in impeccably accented English. I wasn't really all that hungry but I agreed to get out of the crowds. The boy had the same expression as just about every other Indian boy I saw in Goa. Open, honest, energetic, determined, bright, focused in the moment. This lad had more energy than most though, as he berated me with questions about England and how I was liking Goa, with seemingly genuine interest. We soon found ourselves in a welcomingly spacious cafe/diner, a haven from the crowds outside. I crammed myself onto a bench as the boy enthusiastically set directly opposite, along with another, leather faced older man, who had suddenly appeared. I was in no mood for any more games though, and this was beginning to look like another Mumbai-style 'con'. So I ordered a coke, and went into a polite, calm shut-down mode.

Undeterred, the boy continued to pretend to be my best friend in Goa, as the older man, perhaps his father, looked on in knowing resignation of a failed job. I settled up and found myself back in the crowds, needed to get out, so I asked the boy the whereabouts of the nearest internet cafe. Music to his ears. Like a well trained guide-dog, he navigated me smoothly through the maze of stalls and back-alleys and back out into the main street, towards a clapped-out husk of a multi story office block. My reflexes stopped me dead in my tracks as my sense of trouble kicked-in, but then I noticed the comings and goings of others on the steps before us, so I made my way up the tight, unstable stairwell.

Eventually, after many a close call on the stairs, and encouraged by the boy, I was met with the wild, curious eyes of a room full of locals as I emerged, lurching almost doubled-over from the tiny, tight doorway. The boy led me over to what looked to be the only available space in the packed 'Internet-cafe' with its child-sized wooden seats, and again I somehow squeezed my cumbersome frame in. I felt like a giant amongst a children's playschool, and almost completely ill at ease. Forgetting why I was here in the first place, I humoured the technology for a while, which was even worse than back in Calangute, toy-like even, but my immediate problem was the boy and the elder, who peered over the wooden divider at me, unflinchingly watching my every move, I could almost feel their gaze on me as I tried to ignore them in vain.

Scrambling back out of the 'Internet Cafe', I picked up the pace a little in an effort to politely lose them, I was doing ok here, no panic like back in Mumbai, no exchange of funds and now I had my bearings. But this was their turf, and as I ploughed back through the crowds of the market they had caught up again. Cards on the table time, with the stand-off being at a convenience store amongst the market, and the old man claiming they had successfully completed a 'tour' of Mapusa for me, to which I rejected with a laugh and a sigh.

I wasn't backing down here, I was wise to it now, but I entertained them for a little while longer. In the end I bought the boy a Sprite on my own terms, out of my own kindness and because, just like the lad in Cafe Day yesterday, I admired his attitude. I'll never forget the look of pride the elder guy had for the boy as I handed over the bottle, a look only a father could give to his son, and we left it there as I made my way back to the coach terminus.

No signs, tannoys or maps here. All I could do was listen out for the cry of 'Anjuna' and hope. In fact, I had no idea if the coach even went back to Anjuna from here. Thankfully though, as the dusty heat was beginning to take its toll, I could faintly make out similar mutterings in the distance, and as luck would have it, I also noticed the ticket inspector from our outgoing journey dangling out of the door like a monkey on a climbing frame. I joined the queue which looked much too large to fit onto one small coach and turned back to the opening in the wall leading through to the market. The boy was stood there beaming at me, with his newly acquired bottle of Sprite in one hand and waving at me with the other. I had just enough time to wave back as a sudden wave of sadness came over me. This here was a very bright lad, multi-lingual, streetwise, on the ball. I wondered what sort of future he would have in this town. Maybe a childhood spent in the market did him good, but it seemed such a waste of his obvious intelligence and talent. Back home he would've really been someone, but as the coach pulled away my final hope was that he could at least hold onto his positive attitude for as long as possible.

Chapter 6 : What am I doing here?

I was now well into my first week in Goa. Anjuna was lifeless and empty, so I beat the path through the trees and over the bridge into Baga and onto Calangute every day in search of a stimulus, a distraction from the fading dream of building a new life here. I thought I had it all worked out; Rent out my flat back home, and with the proceeds get a modest place by the beach, it was so cheap here I wouldn't need much expendable income, and I could even use the guitar, or teach Karate if I needed or wanted to make a bit of extra cash. The fact was though, there was no live music scene in Calangute, not this time of year anyway, and who was I kidding?, nobody was interested in Karate here, not least from a relative novice like me. So I sampled the bars and restaurants in quiet contemplation, but drinking and dining alone didn't sit right with me, I'd never been the type to initiate a conversation with a stranger, feeling uneasy that I may be bothering someone. So I just used the time to think. What was I doing here? A question I was beginning to struggle with more each day. Here, most people, especially the ex-pats, tended to just 'exist' day by day, no goals, no progression, nothing to build upon or strive towards each day. I hated to admit it to myself, but I was starting to miss home and all the little things associated with it. Technology, modern shopping malls, cleanliness, English pubs, the cool breeze of the sea, but more than anything, back home I always had something to do, somewhere to go, or someone to see. Here, I had to force myself into doing something.

One morning I took the bull by the horns and made my way down to Anjuna Beach at the crack of dawn, I'd not trained in a week and wanted to establish some sort of regime for the remainder of the trip. I'd read that Anjuna was the location of Goa's best nightclub and market, but sadly I'd saw no sign of either throughout my trip. I had to make up my own entertainment. As soon as my foot hit the sand, I was swamped by droves of young children selling jewellery, asking my name and hassling me in general. I tried my best to ignore them and proceeded to a flat looking part of the beach that looked good to train on. Suddenly I heard a young but authoritative voice screech out from the adjoining huts I'd came across on the first day. The crowd immediately dispersed around me as the boy confidently approached me. On the face of it, the boy, no more than an early teen, with relatively smart clothes and hair, looked innocent, but by the way the others fled, almost in fear, I quickly came to the conclusion he must be a superior to them in some way, or at least had some sort of control over them, an enforcer maybe, as ridiculous as that sounds. Regardless, we now stood alone on the beach, a stand-off almost. He had an unnerving aura of self-confidence which almost made me nervous, and also the best English I'd heard so far. Strangely, all he did was ask my name, before going on to tell me about his background and family. The conversation developed into his education and hopes for the future in a similar vein to the coffee shop boy a few days earlier, before going onto the much darker subject of the corrupt government. Not once did he ask me for anything, he just wanted to know about me, where I was from, what I did for a living, what it was like in the west. I'd done it again I thought, I'd jumped to conclusions, I'd thoroughly enjoyed talking to him and that should of been the end of it, but as he walked back over to his hut dwelling, past the twenty or so other children that fled earlier, the look of fear in their eyes and the now deserted beach left me with the feeling that all was not what it seemed. There was a pecking order in place, not just here, I'd seen it around Calangute beach too. Maybe it was something as innocent as family structure, maybe the beaches were monitored by (very) young staff, but something about the situation, fuelled by my inner prejudices made me feel like there was some sort of organised crime at work, maybe even slavery.

I'd almost forgotten about the training, but I found a nice flat area of sand in front of some of the young stragglers sat on some dunes behind me. They remained subdued, so I just started off my training routine while they watched. That was the thing with Karate, it focuses the mind, which was something I was lacking on this trip. It was a beautiful spot, a narrow beach and crashing waves looking out into the massive expanse of the Indian Ocean, but it was overcast, not just the weather, my thoughts were also clouded with thoughts of the children behind me. I was being watched, but was I being monitored? where had the boy gone?, are others on their way? I tried to concentrate as I progressed onto some drills and Kata, but my feet were beginning to sink into the too soft sand. Not only was this not a good place for training, it also felt like an unwelcoming place, a place I didn't belong. So I packed up and headed off, never to return. But just as I was about to exit the beach, the young boy appeared again, this time in a much less than inquisitive mood. "Can you give me your sandals?" he said, with his crowd of followers looking on in the distance. I looked down at my £6 sandals from George@ASDA, reminding myself of the gulf between our countries and cultures. "Of course I will", I'll drop them off on my last day". We smiled and shook hands, while the tension seemed to lift from the rest of the group.

Anjuna Palms seemed even more quieter than usual. I was rapidly coming to the conclusion that there was nothing to do here or even in the whole of Goa. Nowhere to go and no-one to talk to. Another walk into Calangute ? not today. I didn't even have the energy at the moment to attempt anything else. The heat was beating me down, I was getting bored, I was covered in mosquito bites, I was taking malaria tablets which were giving me horrendous stomach cramps, I missed home, I was wondering what I was even doing here. To occupy myself, I decided to go through the documents and books I'd brought with me. On opening the drawer of the desk in my room I noticed what looked like a piece of string. As I reached out to grab it, it wriggled away into the innards of the desk as I leaped out of the way in panic. I stood frozen, eye-balling the desk, what was it, a snake ?, some sort of reptile's tail? either way I couldn't rest until it was out. I began by tentatively nudging the desk with my foot, as my hands were still quivering in shock. This produced nothing, so I kicked the desk harder. A scurrying sound could now be heard, the faint pitter-patter of tiny feet. My mind was now playing tricks, What sort of devilish creature was this? was it dangerous?, poisonous? deadly? With one last violent, nervous kick I shook up the desk again, lifting it off its legs. A large grey rat slithered out of the woodwork with its long tail and a panicked expression similar to my own, shooting straight past me almost under my legs and out through the gap in between the wooden doors. I took a long, deep breathe.

As I began to calm down, I'd noticed it was almost dark outside, From the grounds behind the hostel, a combination of singing/praying had commenced at an ungodly high volume. Almost instantly repetitive, the droning, hypnotic ramblings carried on without respite as I checked over my mosquito bites. My arms and legs were in bad shape, something needed to be done about them soon, Felix had fitted some sort of electronic contraption to the wall which you slotted a 'mosquito deterrent tablet' into, and it sort of buzzed and was supposed to get rid of them. No chance. As I looked at it disappointingly, I noticed swarms of insects of all shapes and sizes had made their home on the ceiling amongst a bed of leaves, larvae, carcasses and cobwebs, I was just about ready to flip, rolling up a copy of Guitarist Magazine, and flailing about out of reach of my unsuspecting room-mates. A large alien-cricket-type creature, about half the size of my hand, hovered into the range of my frenzied attack. The first hit was a glancing shot, stunning the xenomorph enemy into a cobweb by the side of the wall. I showed my pray no mercy as the second blow crushed and split the insect clean in two, splattering deep red blood over the wall and over me. Shaking at the amount of blood and level of violence I swept the remains off the wall and back under the door. The evening stomach cramps were kicking in again, but worse than ever now. Standing up was even out of the question, all I could do was slump onto the bed.

And that's where I stayed, As the music pounded on and the ineffective mosquito buzzer buzzed. I looked around me, a single bed, an ex-rodent home and chair in the corner, a battered un-secure wooden door with gaping gaps and holes, my clothes and suitcase strewn on the floor in the opposite corner, the land-based insect infested filthy stone floor, the airborne insect and spider infested ceiling, the throbbing sores and lumps all over my body, the crippling abdominal pain and the dusty spices polluting the air and tightening my asthmatic wind-pipes. I was a beaten man, physically and emotionally, and I didn't want to be here anymore. There was nothing for me, no way to train, to play. Upping sticks to stay was out of the question, I'd reached boredom in a week already. As I finally relaxed myself enough to sleep and the music faded away, I asked the question again….

What am I doing here?

Chapter 7: Panjim (Part 1)

I woke early in a cold, refreshing sweat. As if the toxins were leaving my body. The stomach cramps had dulled for now, but I knew it wouldn't last. Yesterday was a bad day, but today, somehow I felt strong, determined. Perhaps I'd hit rock bottom and the only way was up from here. Looking up at the roof, the collection of small insects minding their own business didn't seem so bad, didn't bother me as much. I was just a visitor here after all. I decided there and then that today was the comeback, a day of settling in and making the most out of my time here. There was a list of tasks building by the minute at the back of my mind as I got to my feet. First of all was the malaria tablets, which I promptly deposited into the bin. No more stomach cramps. Next, I set about the mess of clothes strewn about the floor, putting the used items in a plastic bag and the rest back in the case. Next up was all the documents, my passport and reading matter I'd brought with me, which were filed away neatly in the desk drawer. I'd almost forgotten about the rat the night before, maybe it was an overreaction but today I felt totally different. Today I felt 'together' and ready for anything. And there you had it. A completely tidy room. Great start I thought, but even better than that was the space I'd created, just enough to train in. With a smile I began the stretching routine there and then, the smooth stone floor being just about the perfect surface to train on.

After I'd pushed myself just enough for the first session, I decided to keep riding this new wave of positivity, the shower room was just down the terrace a few metres away, It was still very early, so I spent a while washing away the doubts of the previously few days. Today I'd visit Goa's capital: Panjim (in English), and from there I promised myself I'd try somewhere different every day. I'd got myself into a rut trailing the path from Anjuna to Baga (and Calangute) each day, clearly we were still in off-season so I needed to try something else. As I made my way out of Anjuna Palms, Felix's wife stopped me midway down the path. You couldn't miss her really, she was a tall woman with a ridiculously large dark perm, huge spectacles ,bright colourful clothing and an even brighter smile.

She asked me how I was enjoying Goa in her usual cheery manner, to which I lied I was having a fabulous time. She offered to do my laundry, another step in the right direction. Tick. I also took the opportunity to ask her about a place to train, the room was ok, but not big enough to practice Kata. She looked up inquisitively at a half finished concrete building just to our right, without a roof, but a flat concrete ceiling of the first floor, and staircase leading up to it from the side. I enthusiastically bounded up the steps, revealing a large flat square area. From up here I could see quite a bit of Anjuna, even some of the path down to the beach, it didn't look too bad at all. I managed a smile of approval at Felix's wife and her young son who had appeared below, I was going to love training up here.

First stop, Mapusa. The coach ride was just as exhilarating as before, but now I felt in the groove and more able to calmly observe my surroundings, taking in the changing scenery from dense undergrowth to vast open farmland and through various pockets of activity, neighbourhoods and commercialism. I loved to people watch, wondering about a group of old men chatting over a drink in a nearby cafe as the coach whizzed past them. Where they that different to me ?

Mapusa. No market today, but a definite plan; Find the connecting coach to Panjim. As I stood in the blistering early morning heat, I was completely lost again, just like last time, as I looked helplessly at the fleets of coaches huddled up in front of the terminus. No timetable here, just dust-ridden, heated, frenzied chaos amongst a deafening barrage of clapped-out engines and faint shouting. I was reminded of my confusion over the name Mapusa, pronounced Map-sa as opposed to Ma-poo-sa, so I listened out for something even vaguely resembling Pan-jim. No such luck, nothing even close. I was met with mostly blank expressions when I asked for directions, but eventually was pointed in a direction towards the edge of the terminus. I tried to shut out the noise, focussing on the driver's assistants calling out various unfamiliar destinations, even just a name beginning with the consonant p. Faintly I heard it…. P….Pan….. so I followed my nose. Panj… Pan-je! Well, close enough. I was now on the coach to Panjim, or Panaji to give it its original name, but pronounced Pan-je, At least I hoped that was my destination.

As the road to Panjim opened out onto a modern motorway, the first I'd seen here, I was shocked. Large buses and trucks screaming past tiny mopeds from both sides. Indians appeared to use mopeds to transport just about anything. Washing machines, tables, even their whole family, some of them riding on the handlebars with no crash-helmets to be seen, anywhere. Lorries casually losing their loads with no-one batting an eyelid. In a word, carnage. Gladly we eventually came to an expansive river with a sleek looking bridge and over into Panjim station. This was my first taste of severe overcrowding, as I had to force my way out of the bus, and through a terminus/market that put Mapusa to shame and was thankfully a lot cooler than outside. Eventually, herded by the crowds out of the station, I came across an unassuming local cafe/restaurant. As I walked in I was overwhelmed by the authenticity of the place. No concessions to tourists here and no over-polite waiter service, this was, by the looks of the clientèle, the coach-drivers choice. I wasn't greeted, but also wasn't made to feel unwelcome. I was merely here to eat, and I sort of liked that. So I just found a space, on large table covered with grotty but colourfully patterned English cafe-style plastic sheets. My co-eaters didn't seem to be conversing with each other anyway. I noticed the lack of cutlery, the technique being that you used a chapati to scoop up the rest of the dish and to mop up afterwards. Rumour has it the right hand is for eating and the left hand is for wiping your behind, but don't hold me to that one. The smell of the place was singing with dense exotic spices and fresh herbs, which made my mouth water, but I hadn't a clue what to order. Some groups had an assortment of dishes laid out, Thali style, some were indulging in typical looking runny curry dishes. I was handed a menu without a word and guessed by the number of people sitting with delicious-looking pots of rice that the most popular dish in the restaurant was Biryani. Glancing at the menu, some of it mercifully in English, there was a whole section devoted to Biryani. Mutton, mutton on the bone, chicken, chicken on the bone and a whole host of other options that have faded from memory. I felt re-assured I was making the right choice here, but as I ordered mutton on the bone Biryani I had no idea that this would be, by far, the most

35

delicious meal I'd ever tasted, and would never taste anything like it again outside of India.

Before it arrived, the completely mute but coldly efficient waiter produced, of all things, a knife and fork, which raised a few eyebrows and some hushed rumblings. But in a strange sort of way I felt quietly confident here, I didn't feel like I was being constantly watched like back on the coast. I actually felt like one of them, an individual just off the street with an empty belly, but also, proud to be different, proud to be English. I'd like to believe there was a feeling of mutual respect in that restaurant on that day. I was also presented with what appeared to be a standard accompaniment dish in these parts. A simple plate of small sweet onion bulbs along with lemon slices, an absolutely magical combination of sweet, sour, tartness and smoothness. Indian's just had it, they knew how to cook, an almost spiritual ability to zone in on the parts of the taste-buds that make the most impact.

And then the main event appeared.

I'd had Biryani before back home. It was a rice dish that was cooked with the meat and veg. It was almost always pretty dry and bland, but came with a separate curry sauce. What was presented with me, on the surface, looked vaguely similar, but was served in a brass pot. On closer inspection however, the top layer of rice had hardened, almost forming a thin husk with fragrant, decadent saffron threads inviting me in. I took my fork and self-consciously prodded into it, revealing the most perfectly cooked by still moist rice below the surface, as the steam escaped I was hit by an almost overwhelming dose of herbs and spices that I haven't experienced before or since. Ginger, garlic, chili, cumin, coriander, cinnamon and cloves. Too many to mention, and each playing their own part. I dug in, the dry crunchy upper layer contrasting beautifully with the firm but moist, steaming, fragrant rice of the layer below it. This was not just any rice either, every grain seemed to be imbued with a different colour, texture, or subtle spice variation, aniseed-like cardamom seeds exploded in my mouth as I hungrily made my way through layer upon layer of joy, all held together with an ingredient I'd never heard of before, ghee, or clarified butter. The ghee made the whole dish glisten, coated the rice with the herbs and spices, and, along with the cherry-on-top saffron, made the dish what it was, and put it leagues ahead of any rice dish back home. The almost unbelievably tasty concoction eventually revealed a final dark layer of deeply succulent mutton, which upped the concentration of spice to the point where I had to come up for breathe for a moment to acknowledge the genius of the dish to both myself and my immediate neighbours. I also took a moment to judge just how far removed the dry, bland, unimaginative English biryani was from the real Mccoy. This was a different dish, a different world. It had obviously been put together with great skill and care, and cooked in one pot. Somehow the chef had managed to cook both the rice and the meat perfectly, hadn't dried out the rice and kept all the moisture in, without turning it into rice pudding, but maybe that was all to do with the ghee. Another way I would describe the dishes construction would be a trifle, with three contrasting layers and a surprise waiting at the bottom. The end of the dish was met with great sadness as I desperately scraped the bottom of the bowl in search of one last morsel. I was addicted and wanted more, but judging by the look of mild disgust on the guy sat opposite, it was probably time to go.

Chapter 8: Panjim (Part 2)

No account of Goa would be complete without mentioning the toilets. And what you get here is usually a hole in the ground. If you're lucky, like in this restaurant, you'll get recesses for your feet either side, and if you're very lucky, you'll get a proper flushing toilet basin. Mercifully the aroma of the magnificent food drowned out any stench as I looked puzzlingly at the only other fitting in the otherwise bare washroom. A brass tap, about five inches up from the floor. The location of the tap continued to baffle me for the rest of my trip until it dawned on me this must be to wash your feet.

Back on the path into Panjim center, I was drawn towards the riverside, with its wide pedestrian-friendly pavement, and looked out over the rippling water and morning haze to the distant bank on the opposite side. The architecture and layout of the place felt almost European and quite familiar, but being from Newcastle I'd seen it all before. There was nothing of note here bar a large vessel fitted out as a restaurant. I casually perused the menu almost as an afterthought before moving on. Across the road I noticed a thankfully modern-looking chemist. Time to sort out my ailments. The professional looking lady behind the counter didn't need a diagnosis, the bites were plain to see, almost golf ball in size by now and covering large sections of my arms and legs. She looked at me as though she'd seen my type, the naive traveller, a million times before, and prescribed 'Odomos' cream whilst proclaiming 'No more bites!'. The cream was 100% effective and began working almost immediately in healing the wounds and deterring further attacks. That was the end of my mosquito bite concerns there and then. Ticked off the list.

As I walked the streets of central Panjim, nothing really stood out as I passed the usual line-up of identikit shops, cafes and restaurants that you would see most days in most cities. Poverty was prevalent, beggars with crudely open-severed limbs, or fevered mothers with newborn babies. Think Slumdog Millionaire. This was uncomfortable, uneasy and something I didn't want to see or know about having thankfully been sheltered from it so far in the resorts.

But like the boy on the beach yesterday, there was something dark and sinister about the place, beneath all the vibrancy, colour and welcoming white smiles. I felt more exposed here and was beginning to see the sanctuaries of Anjuna, Baga and Calangute in a new positive light, but I soldiered on in search of something that I hoped would change my gloomy first impression.

The Municipal Gardens, in the usual central location, lined by the usual bars and cafes was predictably underwhelming, as was its most advertised landmark, 'Our Lady of the Immaculate Conception' church, a drab washed out building atop a flight of steps I didn't have the interest (being non-religious) to ascend. And so I carried on walking until I'd exhausted my options and myself, noticing a reassuringly modern, fashionable looking cafe to satisfy my now rampant hunger for another dose of Biryani. It did not disappoint, being every bit as good as before. As I looked around the almost deserted cafe, serious doubts about the whole trip re-surfaced. There was nothing of note in Panjim, no unique stand out features that I hadn't seen before, nothing to hold my interest, no mental stimulus. I surely would have got more out of a visit to the big European cities: Prague, Barcelona, Berlin. Or maybe it was just my westernised programming craving commercialism, a quick fix of vulgar shopping arcades and the latest fads. Maybe Goa was just different, maybe I was just different and we weren't compatible. The many theories and observations bounced around my head like a game of ping-pong, tiring me out, and then it dawned on me what I was forgetting all along. This trip was meant to be an escape from home, an escape from all the self-imposed rules and daily grind. With this new outlook I knew it was time to leave Panjim and get back to base, to give the holiday resorts I'd given up on a second chance.

On my way back to the station I caught up with the comfortably cynical and moronic social media updates in an internet cafe full of serious gamers wired into their virtual world through headsets. I even emailed one of my friends back home with a half-hearted account on uninterested ears, before arriving back at the worryingly much emptier bus-terminus. As the sun started to set in the distance and an eastern dusk approached, I realised it was quite possible I'd missed the last bus, or at least the last bus from Mapusa back home. I knew the 'Mapsa' call very well now though, and boarded the sparsely populated coach with great relief. As we approached Mapusa the light ominously faded further as my day turned into a race against time. We pulled into Mapusa station to a familiar site the world over, the end of the working day, and the last stragglers winding down before the final commute home. The unique feeling of having been on a 'proper day out' washed over me, but more than that, I was really looking forward to getting back to Anjuna, to reset and start again with my healed stomach, skin, and parked anxieties.

As the coach approached the final corner outside the bike hire shop, night had fell into total blackness, with almost the speed of a dimmer switch. I thanked the driver and his endlessly entertaining assistant and was greeted by the usual warm welcome from the rabble over the the road. In that moment it felt like we'd now become friendly acquaintances, as the hard-sell was gone in place of genuine interest about my day. 'Panjim!' I exclaimed with all the bravado of the experienced traveller, to which the response was muted nods and thumbs of approval. Also in that very moment, it felt like I had arrived back home. As I quietly, almost tiptoed passed Felix's front door towards the hostel behind, I got a buzz of excitement about what tonight would bring, the world was my oyster in what was , after all, the party capital of India. As I passed the terrace of the first apartment, the usual empty chair and table was occupied by a western looking guy who I almost ignored in surprise. 'Evening' I said almost hopefully. 'Evening' was the response of the English fellow-lodger.

Chapter 9: Anjuna Introductions

Still taken aback, I Introduced myself to an out of shape, balding, but well spoken young Londoner called Chris. I made the assumption he was probably in the same boat as me, lost and out to sea, so in typical British style I put forward my solution: "Pint" ? To which he responded with a subdued calmness which couldn't mask the relief of actually having someone to talk to. We agreed we'd head off in ten minutes, but as I quickly got ready for my first 'proper' night out in Goa, I could hear activity from next door.

I arrived at the now familiar terrace outside my apartment, which ran the length of the four adjoining rooms. Chris' room was at one end with the shared wash-room and rudimentary kitchen facilities at the other. Functional white plastic tables and chairs added some home comforts and right next door were sat the couple I'd heard earlier. Ronan and Roisin. A good-looking Irish couple clearly in love and looking to explore and relax. Ronan immediately reminded me of Scarface-era Al Pacino. Dark and brooding, the in-control alpha male. while Roisin seemed the more happy-go-lucky, blonde haired, blue-eyed traveller type. They made a great couple, even finishing each other's sentences off as Ronan graciously made the introductions. I was immediately made to feel at ease when I could've just as easily been a thorn in the side of any plans they may of had for peace and quiet together.

As the ten minute deadline approached, Chris arrived at the table and again introductions were made, nothing too heaving, just a name and address for now. I was chomping at the bit , my mouth watering at the prospect of more Kingfisher. But we had one more member to recruit, as a tall statuesque figure appeared from another one of the apartments. Magda was like a fish out of water, a young Russian girl with curly shoulder length red hair and hardly a word of English. She reluctantly joined us, clearly struggling with the three-way onslaught of Queen's English, Irish and Geordie. She did attempt to make some sort of introduction, but as she loudly and dramatically attempted a background story, all we could decipher was her name.

Ronan, Roisin and Magda were all too happy to join myself and Chris as we set off to the pub. The lights were on at Felix's house as we passed but I still felt as though I had to give them a bit of background to the place, as I assumed the title of tour-guide. The stench from Munchies restaurant caught them completely off-guard, but proved a timely icebreaker as they doubled over to the gag-reflex inducing faeces, farmyard and kitchen aroma concoction. I gave them a full heads-up as we approached the bike hire shop, but there was never really anything to worry about here, they were just a friendly bunch of locals who wished us all a pleasant evening as we passed by and hung a right towards the beach. After all the talk of going on an adventure and seeing the world, what it really boiled down to, what I was really in need of, was a bit of company, a decent night out with friends. Maybe that was why things had got off to such a false start. Maybe that was why my thoughts had turned inward towards cultures and prejudice. Maybe that's why, until now, everything had seemed a bit flat.

The road down to the bar was pitch black, with not a soul in sight. I pointed out a few landmarks along the way. The road to Baga, Dum Biryani (another local restaurant) Paradiso, (supposedly the biggest nightclub in Goa, but sadly still closed due to it being off-season). In no time at all the road bended round to the left and we arrived at the Sea Rock bar and restaurant, situated at the end of the road and overlooking the sea. This area was also a gathering place, with other small cafe's, public telephones, taxis and moped activity, but again very quiet at this time of day at this part of the season. As we entered the empty bar, Sea Rock's seemed ill prepared to withstand the monsoon, with its rickety wooden construction and tarpaulin roof completely open to the elements. As we sat down to order, the miserable, walrus-like owner had just finished issuing orders to the usual fresh-faced young waiter, who we all took an immediate shine to. As he took a request for my third biryani of the day, we all discussed our reasons for being here in Goa, or to put it more accurately, of being in Goa in the off-season. In the background the violent action of the film "Rollerball" was distracting me somewhat, I looked forward to watching it properly when I got home.

Chris, as it turns out, was a city-slicker, banker, hedge-fund manager. The type that would go on and cause the financial markets to crash in the coming years. Below the calm exterior he was in meltdown and needed an escape. His honesty was touching, but none of the sharks were watching him here. Here, he was with friends. Ronan and Roisin had it all worked out. Ireland, having just adopted the Euro, was booming. They were both studying to make their fortune in property, met at University, fell in love and were now on an adventure together before the hard work started. Magda told a long drawn out story full of expression to a table full of blank incomprehension. Then it came to my turn......

In 2005 I'd been made redundant after 8 years of becoming progressively de-skilled as an I.T. professional. I'd started from the bottom again in customer services and now worked as a 'Ticketing Consultant' for American Express, which is every bit as bad as it sounds, but I was also out of place and out of time in an office full of young people and an over-the-top camp manager who took an instant dislike to me. Through all of this, including the demise of my band at the time, I was in a relationship I had lost interest in, but was in too deep, as we now lived together. It all culminated on a holiday to the island of Fuerteventura just a few months earlier. One night I just wanted to go out alone so I went to see a band at the 'Rock Island Bar' in Corralejo. I got talking to a guy, first about the band, and then onto what I was doing here without my partner. As it turned out he'd been in the same situation as me, so we chatted about it some more, visited some more bars and eventually he recommended I should go to Goa, play some guitar, and do some karate. I looked up at the half-puzzled, half-suspicious expressions looking back at me, then finished off my story. "I decided there and then I was going to Goa".

As Sonny, the young waiter went about his task with effortless efficiency we revelled in just how inexpensive the place was. 30p (English Sterling) for a Kingfisher beer, even cheaper for shorts. In fact, as the night progressed Ronan was cutting out the middleman and just buying bottles of vodka. I asked Sonny where the toilet was, and he signalled over to behind the bar. I walked through, noticing to my right, a front room, complete with furniture, a blasting TV and an entire family! They glanced over with hardly a stir as I hurriedly, desperately made my way past. The corridor branched right into a kitchen of sorts where I was attacked by wet underwear, slapping my face and entangling me from ridiculously low washing lines. I eventually made it through to the toilet (a hole in the ground with two ridged foot-wells).

Back at the table there were casualties. Chris and Magda decided to call it a night but I stayed on. Roisin was, as Ronan put it, 'cracked'. So he took her home as Sonny looked on in hope. I was his last customer. We'd all tipped him extensively throughout the night but as I looked over to his sleeping bag in the corner, that now familiar feeling of something not being quite right washed over me. I had dutch courage to spare right now, so I politely asked him about his sleeping arrangements. With the walrus looking on, it appeared that Sonny basically ran the whole show, morning, noon and night, sleeping on the floor when, and only when the last person (in this case me), had left. As usual, he fed me a line about this being the foundation onto better things, education, etc. with a smile and determined look, but all I could see was slave labour. Child slave labour. As I left, I couldn't resist a look back. The walrus seemed to be tucking Sonny into his sleeping bag. They were smiling, as if they'd had a good day and were looking forward to tomorrow, and who was I to question that?

Chapter 10 : Cafe Mambo

And so, for the following week at least, we all went about our business. From time to time we'd get together, frequently back at the Sea Rock, or late at night on the terrace over vodka and coke, but largely we kept a respectful distance, not wanting to tread on anyone's toes or get in the way of anyone's plans. I continued to make the almost daily trek into Baga, but just knowing I had company back at the hostel reassured and relaxed me. Finally, I felt comfortable, at home.

The rooftop training picked up pace, with my audience of one, Felix's young son, looking on from below, copying my efforts. With the seemingly endless free-time, I also broke out the acoustic guitar for the first time, and even composed some new songs, sometimes singing and playing completely unbridled, out on the terrace, in full view of the workmen opposite. I was in the groove, in tune at last with my surroundings, content in myself. This daily ritual has now faded into memory. but as the weekend approached, we all decided to visit Calangute that evening, this was to be both a celebration and a farewell before we went our separate ways.

We all gathered once again out on the terrace in our Sunday best. There was anticipation in the air, as well as a touch of sadness, I hadn't got to know them all that well, but it was nice having them around. Ronan, in typical style had already arranged transport and as Felix's wife notified us of the Taxi's arrival, we abandoned the usual vodka and coke bottles littering the flimsy plastic table. Surprisingly (although I was beginning to expect the unexpected here) a half-Jeep, half-truck vehicle pulled up outside Anjuna Palms. Two gangsta-style youths manned it, while we occupied a bench arrangement in the back. As they pulled away the excitement was palpable as we issued request after drunken request to our DJ host, which rapidly degenerated into 'Hips Don't Lie' by Shakira on repeat (my favourite song at the time), along with my trademark loud and over-enthusiastic review of everything that was 'brilliant' about Calangute.

As the party wagon ground to halt at the Calangute crossroads and the exhausted driver and DJ were paid off. The mood changed to a more civilized one as we considered our options for dinner, rapidly coming to the decision that closest was best, we arrived at a uncharacteristically 'Chinese' looking restaurant, complete with dragon decorations and other oriental imagery. As I looked around, Chris, Ronan, Roshin and Magda, we were all so different, individuals from varying backgrounds. Yet we had found ourselves here, right at this moment, in this weird and wonderful place, raising a toast to friends.

After the meal, we went traditional Goa, and onto a beach shack which was really no more than a tarpaulin roof propped up by vertical wooden beams. A lone fridge served as a bar, seating being the usual white plastic table and chairs. We all took a seat and drink as people of all ages danced to the music in total abandon with trademark wide white smiles. Us westerners remained stoic, cradling our bottles nervously as the dancing, already hilariously intentionally terrible, degenerated further into clumsy acrobatics and general fumbling about in the sand. With a knowing smile, I was once again reminded of why I loved India and Its people so much. There was no trouble here, no egos, jealousy or conflict. in fact nothing serious or negative at all. Time after time we were asked to get up and join in, but we were all just too full-up with food and drink by now. That was except for Magda, who appeared a lot younger than us and seemed to be getting a bit distracted and in need of mixing with her peer-group of young Russians we noticed back at the the Sea Rock. The journey to the toilet was every bit as bizarre, a maze of military equipment this time, following by the usual hole in the ground.

As the "dinner and drinks" Part 1 of the evening plan drew to a close, it was time to initiate "Part 2 – Cafe Mambo". After almost a week of singing its praises, I'd finally broken them down. We'd head back to Anjuna first for a quick change (mostly for the benefit of the girls) and then to Calangute's/Baga's best club. As the taxi pulled up outside Anjuna Palms, the still distracted Magda, instead of going back to the hostel, headed straight, without a word, in the direction of the Sea Rock. That was the last we ever saw of her. As we gathered in the taxi to head back into Baga, we concluded it must have been the language barrier, or in true Mowgli fashion, 'wanting to be with her own kind'.

Tito's Lane, Baga was the epicentre of Calangute/Baga (or probably even Goa) night-life. It lead down to Baga beach from the main Calangute/Baga road with Cafe Coffee Day on the corner. I'd stayed clear of the more famous Tito's so far, it just seemed a bit too exclusive or, to be blunt, ponsy. I much preferred Mambo's which was situated just further down and extended out onto the beach itself. Mambos was every bit the bar/club I'd hoped to find in Goa, The modern central bar served you just about any drink or food you liked, all hours of the day and night. Moving away from the bar were crowds of revellers amongst wooden totem-pole structures and palm trees, Just like the internet cafe back in Anjuna, the decor almost had a Jamaican flavour to it, Indeed, the odd spliff-toting rastafarian was a common sight here.

As we took our seats on the outskirts of the dancefloor/main-standing area, we observed the strange courting rituals of the locals. Public displays of affection were a strict no-no it seemed here in Goa. Not once did I see a couple even holding hands. Instead we witnessed, testosterone fuelled, tight-shirted males, dancing like peacocks in a frenzy literally inches in front of their prey's nose. As the men vastly outnumbered the women, almost 10 to one, women got in for free, and were obvious targets for the duration. The most attractive of them would, quite naturally, instigate a dance-off between 2 or even 3 suitors at a time. Although there was never any trouble, one thing's for certain. I would have hated to be a single woman in Goa (or loved, whatever floats your boat).

As we watched, drank and chatted, various domestic animals would emerge from under the seats. Cats, Dogs, the odd Parrot. This place was devoid of all the suffocating rules necessary to maintain order back home. Here, you just did what you liked, free to enjoy the moment. We discussed their plans, Chris was off on the sleeper train to New Delhi, while Ronan and Roshin were off for some private time to a beach shack along the coast in Colva. As for me, as I looked out onto the idyllic beach and over the Indian Ocean to back home, there was only one place for me right now, and that was right here.

Chapter 11: Down a Hole

Today was everyone's last day in Goa apart from mine. I donned my tour-guide hat one last time to take them to Panjim, via Mapusa as always. The mood on the coach was melancholic. We'd formed a bond as the aliens in a foreign land and knew we probably wouldn't see each other again. As we disembarked onto the streets of Goa's Metropolis, we couldn't escape the fact that we'd drawn attention to ourselves. Even amongst our own group was a variety of looks, cultures, fashions, and even languages. From the squat, duck-out-of-water, smart businessman on holiday; Chris, to the fashion-model tall, super-trendy and impressionable Magda. The chilled out antipodean-style traveller Roisin, to the dark, brooding leader with all the machismo and looks of a Hollywood movie star (Ronan).

As we headed out of the station towards the place I first tasted biryani, a cold-sweated panic hit me like a train, as I fumbled around my many pockets. My wallet was gone! As I started to freak out, the party looked on, motionless on the street, as if waiting for their next instruction. I had to see them off there and then, to go after my only option of going back to the bus that dropped us off. After all the politeness and friendship, it was a terse goodbye, I'd brought them all here, and embarrassingly, after all my hyping of Panjim, I'd have to leave them in the lurch. I did a 180 straight back to the station, at double quick march.

Crushingly, Panjim station was now more heaving than ever. I had no idea of what the coach looked like amid the kaleidoscope of paint-jobs and chintz. I tried to start off vaguely at the spot we were dropped off at, but it was hopeless. I searched a couple of nearby coaches mostly out of desperation but I knew my wallet was long gone by now. Luckily I found enough loose change to get me back home. I took a breath and weighed up the options.....

All my travel money was now gone, along with my wallet, which also contained my debit card, but luckily I still had my credit card back at the hostel. The only question was, could I use it over here? I looked back towards the river into Panjim. Maybe I should just catch up with the others, even just to say a proper goodbye. I had more pressing issues though, I needed to cancel my missing debit card, immediately. The last of money was spent on the coach ride home, which seemed to take an age. At this moment I had no idea how I was going to get through this crisis, but step one was definitely get back to the hostel. I hurtled past Felix's place and began rifling through my documents and belongings. I found 200rs and a credit card.

I stormed out of Anjuna palms and flashed past the bike shop almost on autopilot, towards the nearest phone box just by the Sea Rock. It was a dry, blazingly hot day, which did nothing to cool my temperature or lower my rising blood pressure. I hurriedly and clumsily picked up the phone in the makeshift phone kiosk, I had all the Barclays contacts numbers laid out before me, which I'd luckily took away with me just in case. The first obstacle was actually getting through to the U.K., which I eventually fathomed out, and got through to the comfortingly familiar accent of a bank call-center clerk. Card cancelled, I stood outside for a while in the dusty street amongst the taxi's, pondering the next move. I needed more funds, a cashpoint machine and the correct pin number which at this moment I wasn't 100% sure of. There was a hotel half way back up the road to Anjuna Palms which seemed relatively modern, so I brazenly walked up to reception and simply asked the question. This was make or break time, either the smartly dressed man behind the counter helped me or I was basically stranded.

Just like the man in the kiosk on my first day in Anjuna, I was calmed down and made to feel at ease by the hotel receptionist. A simple question of "How much do you need?" and a signature, no pin required. Sure, they got a pretty high commission for their trouble, but yet again the Goan people had taken me by surprise. I was in deep trouble 5 minutes ago. Now I was back in the game.

The morning's panic and the heat had taken its toll as I drifted off into a deep comfortable sleep. It was getting dark by the time Roisin and Ronan returned, sadly not accompanied by Chris and Magda who had now gone off on their separate journeys. We sat at the table outside one last time and toasted to a moment in time we'd never forget, then just as the darkness fell I noticed a green beam of light in the distance, over by the Sea Rock. Re-invigorated by the long sleep, I promptly excused myself and headed in its direction.

The light looked to be behind the Sea Rock, almost on the beach in the dense forest. I could now also hear crowds of people, and faint music, was this the start of the high season? Was this the first of the legendary Goa Beach parties? I was uncontrollably drawn to the strobing green light like a magnet as it rotated up into the sky in time with the music. There seemed to be no other route to it other than the path behind the Sea Rock into complete blackness. I didn't care though, as my destination loomed into view. A large whitewashed villa adjacent to the beach. Cars were pulling up outside, well dressed party goers, with modern dance music pumping inside. I paused for a moment. Maybe this was a private party? The clientèle was certainly a class above what I'd seen so far. Either way though, I decided to take a closer look, but as I stepped forward I lost my footing in the blackness, and felt myself falling. Time slowed down exponentially as my flailing arms and legs searched in vain for a branch or the ground. As the impact eventually came, I froze for a moment to take stock. I was now perched on some sort of concrete ledge. As my eyes adapted to the darkness I could see that I'd landed on the end of some sort of sewer. I thanked my lucky stars the ledge had broken my fall, as the bottom was a good ten feet or so further down, which would have meant a broken leg at best. As I hesitantly moved my limbs, everything seems to be in one piece, and there was little pain, but maybe I was just in shock. I eventually got to my feet to realize my next problem. The top of the sewer was just out of reach. I'm no climber, being heavy and clumsy, but I do (so I'm told) have a very loud voice. So, from the sewer in the darkness I decided I had no option but to call for help. My sheer Britishness, even now, made me consider what exactly *to* shout out in desperation. I settled for a HEEEEEELLLLLLPPPPP!!!!

I listened out for the response, but all I could hear was the party in the distance, with the waves crashing in the background, maybe the tunnel was blocking the sound, I called out again and again this time with more urgency. Nothing. I now had faith in the Goan people, so far they'd always popped up just at the right time, but not this time.

My heart sank. I cried out a final time, and the force of the air through my battered ribcage took away my remaining energy. I sunk back onto the ledge and must've blacked out for a time.

The building, rhythmic sounds of the party jolted me back into the real world. I needed to get out and no-one was here to help. I paused a little to focus on the top the sewer, and, just as a practice run, reached up to grab the edge. Not too bad I thought as I pulled myself up from the ledge a little and then back down again. I psyched myself up with deep breathes and visualized the ascent. Reach up, pull up, leg up and push... over and over in my head. With one last deep breath I went for it, reaching up with both hands. I knew I couldn't hold it for long so from under me, my feet scrambled up, just about gripping the damp concrete of the sewer interior. Now the really difficult bit, with one lung-busting heave, I pushed up again with both hands to give my foot a chance to make it from waist height to the top of the wall. I just about managed to hook it on the edge. I paused for a second to catch my breath again. The worst was over as I now had three limbs holding me up. With one last final push I managed to swivel over the top of the sewer, landing in a heap in the dark undergrowth.

As I emerged from the path outside the Sea Rock and into street lighting I hesitantly checked over the damage. I was badly grazed below the knee but nothing much else, superficially. But as the cold night air brushed on shivering skin and through to my battered bones, I could feel a quivering inside. I'd been knocked. Shaken up, Inside and out. Slowly and painfully I made my way back to Anjuna Palms. I'd had a lucky escape.

As though nothing had happened, I re-took my seat beside Roisin and Ronan and nonchalantly poured a vodka and coke with quivering hands, only to be met with worried astonishment. I noticed my elbows had also taken a bit of a beating as they took me through the damage report. A gash on the cheek, and a badly cut up ankle. As they scrambled for a solution to make me feel better, I had only one, as the nausea began to kick in. "I'm off to bed. Goodnight".

Chapter 12 : The High Season Begins.

I should have felt a lot worse as the blinding light of a new morning pierced through the makeshift window of my room, jerking me out of my slumber. Maybe I was lucky to be alive, or at least glad that there were no broken bones, or even a bruised/pulled muscle, but I felt great today. As I headed for the wash-room I noticed a book on the table outside. A political, sci-fi thriller which Roisin was raving about and she'd kindly left behind for me. On my return home, we'd speak again via email, where she'd reminisce about her and Ronan listening to my playing and singing efforts outside on the terrace. They really were a great couple, but now, here in my last week in Goa,I was once again Anjuna Palm's sole resident.

As I showered away the grime and darkness of yesterday's events, what I was left with was merely a collection of superficial cuts and grazes, which were already healing up, as if the very atmosphere of the place was attacking my wounds. I bounded out of the hostel down to the familiar path to Baga. The rains had stopped, but something else felt different. I could sense a buzz about the place. As my momentum tumbled me down the ramp of Baga bridge, a Jeep loomed into view and screeched to a halt almost at my feet. "Where's the Party?" Said a young Asian looking woman with a BIG Afro just like Felix's wife. The shrug of my shoulder's didn't seem to dampen their spirits as the Jeep continued on up the road towards Anjuna. This was it then, the start of the high season, and tourists were arriving.

My first stop of the day was Brittos, a beach-side cafe in Baga. I was early and the place was just about empty, bar an English ex-pat. I suppose he represented everything I came here for. He was living the lifestyle and was openly comfortable in his surroundings as he read his morning paper, probably the same paper in the same spot every morning. The man, probably in his late 40's, was tanned and bespectacled with long grey dreadlocks, shorts and sandals and didn't seem to have a care in the world. I wondered what his story was, perhaps an ex-teacher by the look of the way he studied his broadsheet. As I tucked into my full English though, I saw another side to him. The dreadlocks really didn't suit him, he looked out of place, in the no-man's land between being a tourist and a native. In that moment, I realised I couldn't live here the way he did. However much I'd fallen in love with the place, I was English and this was India, end of. I settled back into my chair, Brittos was a spacious, airy place with naval and subterranean décor that reminded me of fish restaurants back home. All blue and white livery accessorised with ropes and buoys. As I gazed out at the fabulous view of the Indian Ocean I felt an itchy sensation on my scabbed-up wound under my knee. Flies! and lots of them, swarming around the salty crust and nibbling away, ignoring any attempt to remove them. I made a flustered getaway.

Back in central Calangute, I headed for a 24 hour food/drink complex and a modern looking bar on the second floor. All the trademark Indian-isms were present and correct. The friendly and highly motivated barman, the obsession with the west, the life threatening electrical work, and amusingly a flat-screen TV, mounted on the wall, but with the power supply dangling about underneath, connected to the socket by the floor. A good effort nonetheless. I attempted to relax on the square bean-back style seats and super-low table, but I was just not built for such an arrangement. Nevertheless I peered out onto the courtyard below, all hustle and bustle, with my pint of Kingfisher in hand. I was beginning to feel isolated again. There was no way into these people's lives unless I forced myself upon them, something I wasn't willing to put them through. The mental stimulus of the gang back at Anjuna Palms was missing and once again I had nothing to do, nowhere to go, nothing to see and no-one to talk to. I wondered how the man back at Britto's coped. It was now becoming a chore just to fill out the long, empty days. I continued drinking and self-analysing.

Next, I found myself in what was billed as an 'English Pub', hidden away across the street. It was tiny, dark, empty apart from the barman who didn't utter a word, and devoid of any character or atmosphere whatsoever. I finished the pint almost immediately before finding myself back on road to Baga, dizzied by the alcohol, desperately in search of something to relieve the ominous onset of boredom which was sobering me up.

I decided to brave the super-persistent beach-touts to break up the scenery and strolled back towards Mambo's as the sun was beginning to set. The shoreline was animated by the usual violently crashing waves which couldn't break my contemplation mode. Maybe I had just arrived too early in the year, but I really wanted to experience Goa in high season. As I took up a wicker sofa on the beach-side terrace of Mambo's I resigned myself to a lonely and fairly repetitive last few days. The early promise this morning hadn't come to fruition and the flies were at my knee again as I tried to relax and order a curried fish dish and a kingfisher.

My tea arrived and yet again Goa surprised me. I was presented with two bland looking pieces of fish, but cooked so simply on the bone over a fire, covered in a curry paste and coated in crispy breadcrumbs. The perfect snack food to soak up yet another beer. The vista into the sunset over the open ocean was now almost achingly beautiful, The amber sun bathing the whole place in a warm glow while the palms trees cast longer and longer shadows. I was captivated yet again and made to forget about such triviality as 'being bored' in favour of a much more agreeable 'just being'. Of all the sunset's I experienced in Goa, this one stayed with me the longest.

Familiar accents snapped me out of my daydream, as I noticed the place filling up, and the atmosphere change almost immediately from calm and quiet to the excitement of the weekend. Looking around at the crowds of customers stood around me as I remained sprawled out too comfortably on the sofa beneath them, I was no longer out of place. these were people of my age and culture, dressed like me, laughing and joking. At last!

I felt an uncontrollable urge to get back to Anjuna, get ready and get back out here for a night out. One Taxi ride later I found myself outside Munchies, the restaurant outside Anjuna Palms. It was absolutely jumping. There were no English people here though, as It turns out the place was full of Israelis. As usual, I pulled up a chair, ordered and observed them. I'd heard that Anjuna was popular with the Israelis, that they were loud, with massive egos, aggressive even. The rumours appeared to be true as the alpha-males, who made even Ronan seem effeminate, bellowed and boasted. I wasn't arguing, these were tough-as-nails looking soldier types no doubt hardened by years of conflict back home. They were simply letting off steam and their squaddie style antics kept me highly entertained until my second favourite dish of all time was presented to me.

Butter Chicken, I can still taste it now. The most luxuriously comforting, moreish tasty curry in the whole world. After one spoonful I was hooked. The sweetness of a korma but with more of a kick.... I greedily tucked in, eager to get back down to Mambo's. A quick shower, change and taxi later, and I was back on Tito's Lane. Forget about Mambo's. There was a sea of people outside Titos and who was I to miss out. As I paid the extortionate entry fee and entered a world of chrome, neon and darkness. I slumped drunkenly into a nearby chair. I was beyond speech as the dense crowds blurred around me and made the room spin. Here I was, the high season, in Goa, too drunk to stand or even raise my head, feverishly picking away at the itchy scab on my knee, bleeding and muttering away to myself.

Completely partied out.

Chapter 13: Candolim, Crumbland and the River Princess.

The morning light jerked me into consciousness with all too familiar and somewhat comforting hangover symptoms. As I got to my feet I could still feel the alcohol coursing through my veins and beating a painful rhythm around the side of my head. I was fully up to speed, in the saddle and relishing another day of absolute freedom and adventure. My ailments just came with the package.

As I once again made my way down to the bike shop on the corner, all my daemons and anxieties had been left behind. Goa had fulfilled its promise to the full and now everyday was just a bonus, extra icing on top. Home-time was looming and there was no way I wasn't going to make the most the last few days. To the bike-shop attendant's obvious and palpable surprise, I actually stopped at their corner this time, 'Want Bike?' absolutely!

Confusingly, there were no bikes, instead, another short stocky man I hadn't noticed before appeared from inside the tiny blue shack, the thick meaty smell of cannabis almost burning my lungs. He was dressed much smarter than the rest of them, who resembled a pack of stray dogs, and had a business-like character about him. Commandeering one of the regular's mopeds, he ushered me onto the back seat. Cash in hand and completely befuddled, I hopped on.

We sped off down the usual trail to Baga but suddenly turned off in a new direction as dark thoughts and alarm bells threatened to ring once more. The clean, modern residential area was much like the one I and Felix had stopped off at on day one, and before too long we pulled up outside a large garage of a typical suburban semi. The huge door swung upon to reveal a collection of shiny mopeds. A dark blue Honda Activa had my name on it. Still none the wiser, the quiet but efficient guy (I was guessing he owned the house and the mopeds) switched over to the Honda and once again beckoned me over to ride shotgun, and off we went again, all the way back to the bike shop…

The thing with Goa was, no matter how illogical a situation was, the locals just accepted it and got on with it. This bike renting lark was typical, as I handed over my money to the familiar ancient looking man and the bike owner sped off again, I couldn't even bring myself to make sense of their system, it was just plain silly but no-one seemed to care. The fee was vague, and agreed between them in a huddle, as was the number of days rent, all that mattered was they had their money, and as they all reconvened inside the hut in a cloud of smoke I now had my very own set of wheels.

The destination was set. Candolim, the next town south of Calangute. This time I stuck to the main roads as it seemed easier, and before I knew it found myself on a main highway of sorts, devoid of any safety gear, or even any lessons. It was a vivid, bright day, and as I cranked on the accelerator the refreshing wind made me more even more awake and eager to find out what today had in store. I sped over a bridge of sorts, casually breezing past an official at a checkpoint, he waved at me frantically and authoritatively to stop.

I had bared the speed limit no mind, It was just a moped after all. But the sign, I now noticed, did read thirty, kph as opposed to mph. The hulking policeman paced over calmly and ominously, looking more like a special forces soldier than a bobby. He was armed ,wore a beret, desert camo uniform and, unusually, a ginger crew cut . Tall, heavily muscled and tattooed, I was literally quaking in my boots. "Do you have a licence?" he muttered coldly as he reached into his top pocket for a pen and pad. I didn't of course, didn't think I needed one. "Speed limit is thirty, did you know that?" he continued, with a little more humility and maybe humour in his voice. "Sorry, I didn't know". Without any further ado, he fined me 1000Rs, right there on the spot. Almost gratefully I hurriedly delved into my side-pockets for my wallet and was all too eager to hand it over and get out of there.

Before too long I was on Calangute road again, at a much more cautious pace, and on into Candolim, which continued on from where Calangute left off and shared the same stretch of coast. This was a much more affluent district, with leafy suburbs lining the main strip but not a great deal of bars or shops that I could tell, maybe they were situated closer to the beach. I decided it really wasn't worth stopping yet so I continued all the way to the end. Eventually the road swung to the the left and then in a large circle to the right, past some high end bars and restaurants and onto Aguada Fort, which was spectacularly situated, jutting out to the Arabian sea and overlooking the Mandovi River. As I disembarked and strolled around the spacious ruins, I also noticed a lighthouse in an impressively good condition. This was a well looked after heritage site that the locals were obviously proud of.

Thinking that there wasn't really much else to see I thought I may as well check out the beach, the path led me past a very expensive-looking hotel complex confirming that this place was indeed designed for the well-healed. I peered in through the gates, gawping at the well-cut lawns, palm trees and modern, classy architecture. As I headed to the beach, something you don't see everyday, a huge ship, on first glance a passenger liner, on its side and aground, maybe only a hundred metres away from the shore! I stood in cold shock, maybe even fear, as I watched the waves crash violently against it. I encountered a lot of typically 'Indian' situations on my trip, most of which raised a smile, but what I was witnessing here, I thought, was the aftermath of a disaster, maybe even loss of life. (As I later found out this was the bulk ore carrier "River Princess" which ended up being grounded during the 2001 monsoon). I took a moment to take in the scene of the vast, ugly, angular iron bulk contrasting sharply against the soft shades of the coastline. Very uneasy on the eye, disturbing even.

On my way back I noticed a sign outside the last bar in Baga before the bridge. It simply read "Live Band Tonight: Crumbland". That was tonight's entertainment sorted. Back at Anjuna Palms I went over the day's events with Felix's wife. She was filled with exasperation. First of all the speeding fine had been a con (I really should have known by now). Why didn't I ask for a receipt from the official? I felt good and bad about this, good because I now knew I had free reign on the moped and bad because I was down a tenner, either way it seemed to amuse her. She also gave me the full lowdown on the River Princess, angry that the powers that be hadn't sorted it out by now.

After a rejuvenating few hours kip, the night-out adrenaline rush kicked in once again as I got myself together in the now familiar washroom and polished off a quick biryani and kingfisher at Munchies. I opted to take the moped down the usual path to Baga this time, which was a lot more fun, not to mention dangerous, as I scrambled over the dirt paths and the undergrowth. The journey took no time at all as the usual scenery flashed past, culminating in the kickstart-style obstacle of the Baga bridge, which needed a full-throttle run-up the ramp followed by heavy braking to stop me falling off at the other side.

Another obvious advantage of Goa was the lack of parking laws. I merely screeched to a halt outside the bar, jumped off, dusted myself down, went up to the bar and ordered a beer. The bar itself was lovely inside, with marble and floral decoration everywhere. This was my kind of bar too, nice brass footrest, lots of space, lots of stools, and manned by the most customer friendly people in the world. I took an instant shine to this particular lad, a young teenager inflicted with a slight build, acute shyness, horrendous bucked teeth, and the thickest jam-jar spectacles I'd ever seen. But like every other Goan I'd came into contact with, he hadn't been poisoned by the cynicism and laziness we get back home. Truth be told he was probably the worst barman in the world, spilling drinks, smashing glasses and messing up orders left right and center, but you could tell he was really trying. I was his first customer of the night so I put him at ease by not rushing or stressing him.

Then the owner appeared. A round sweating bull of a man with the look of a mustachioed Italian opera singer. He was gesticulating to everyone and I feared for the young lad, but he was great with him, patiently, gently;showing him the ropes from his obvious years of experience. You just didn't get this sort of thing in England anymore. This guy really cared about his staff and you could tell it was a big night for all of them. As the bar filled the owner greeted everyone personally. As kingfisher after kingfisher went down he would stop the lad from charging me from time to time, on the house, thankful for my custom. He knew how to treat his customers well, and for that he was rewarded with a full bar and captive audience for the 'turn'. Crumbland; who, as it turns out are a four-piece rock band from Finland on a tour of India.

After more frantic organizing by the owner, Crumbland were now set up and ready, with everyone in place, band, bar-staff, owner and punters. To my surprise they played almost exclusively original material, good original material, in a post-Nirvana style. Strangely the audience were completely into the music, even though the set must've been completely new to them. No leaving the bar in disgust or 'Sweet Home Alabama' demands here. The owner had a look of pure satisfaction, looking for all the world like he'd orchestrated a masterstroke as the tills rang and the audience cheered. Crumbland were a great band, led by a charismatic, good-looking front-man who reminded me of clean-cut Johnny Rotten. He was not only accomplished vocally (in a variety of styles), but could also hold his own as a rhythm guitarist, and sometimes lead player. He was the type of person you just had to take your hat off to, he just had it. The Fender Telecaster toting guitarist, in contrast, was more troll-like in appearance, like the brother that got all the bad genes, musically he supported the front-man superbly well although it was obvious who the focal point of the band was. Towards the end of the night he surprised us all with a solo rendition of "Isn't she Lovely" by Stevie Wonder, revealing a crystal clear vocal tone in contrast to the vocalist's grit and grunt. The rhythm section were great too, at one stage breaking into an infectious "Knight Rider" influenced riff that stuck in the memory. The bass player was a tatty blonde haired surf-dude type, complete with a beany hat and the youngest member of the band by some way. Of course, no-one ever remembers the drummer do they?

As the night progressed, the nervous barman gained in stature before my very eyes, expertly mentored and supported by his boss all way, to the point where he even looked like he was beginning to enjoy himself and cracked a smile. The owner was now in full flight, juggling the band, his staff and his punters, which now included entertaining a group of very important (and rich) looking gentleman at the opposite end of the bar to me, maybe business associates of some description. Throughout the night I didn't really engage with anyone except the staff, except for an impressionable English couple who had just arrived in Goa. We didn't really have a lot in common though, they were enamoured with the Goan party scene and had the safety net of each other, the typical British holiday makers naively seeking culture but only on their terms, in their comfort zone. I, however, was reaching the end of my journey, on my own, and had almost emotionally fallen off a cliff, without a safety net, and got back up again. I didn't want to give away any of Goa's secrets though, I wanted them to savour it like I did, and maybe learn from it like I had done, and so as the band finished to a rapturous applause and the crowds drifted towards Mambos, I made my excuses and mingled in with the masses.

Before I left though, I made the effort to thank the boy, and his fantastic boss, for a great evening. The owner grabbed him by the shoulders and shook him with pride, showing him off to his pals at the bar whilst enjoying a well-earned drink with them. This had been a baptism of fire for the boy, and he got through it. I often wonder how far he made it in life. I left just as I began, to an empty bar.

Now much worse for the wear, I'd almost forgotten about the moped still parked outside. I clambered on and caught up with the crowds headed for Mambos. The atmosphere on the streets was electric that night, with people dancing as they waited to get in, or enjoying a snack al-fresco in one of the many take-aways and cafes. I don't think I'd ever felt as free in my life ever, or since. Free of any financial burden (because it was so cheap here), free of laws and regulations, (as I pulled up drunk right outside the nightclub on a moped with no licence or safety gear with no parking fees), and free of anyone making decisions for me. But for all this, as I entered the nightclub and attempted to join in, I was alone, not really part of it. Crumbland had even appeared and were the toast of the town, I was pretty much a nobody.

Mambos had never been so packed out, so much so that I could barely move. After a while the constant jostling and repetitive dance music started to grate enough for me to want to leave. I stumbled out and back onto the moped. After my alcohol riddled body had finally worked out where the headlights were, I tentatively made my way back to Baga bridge. I couldn't chance the main roads in my state, likely I'd end up in prison or dead, my only option was the pitch dark undergrowth. Anything could've happened to me on that journey back, I was a sitting duck with my blaring headlights, a prime ambush target anywhere along the deserted dust paths lined by the blackness of tall trees. The makeshift village half-way back was spookily quiet at this early hour, not one bit welcoming or approving of the noise or bright beams. I didn't know of another way through so I held my breathe and zipped through as quickly as I could.

Eventually the stressful journey came to an end and I found myself approach the bike shop once again. The road was damp and as I turned to head back home I couldn't resist opening the throttle and going for the power-slide, which I pulled off surprisingly effectively and with some style, screeching round the bend in full control to the approving audience of the bike shop crew. Did they ever go to bed?

Chapter 14: Vagator and Chapora

The final three days of this eye-opening, life-changing experience were now before me. I'd done Baga / Calangute to death, and saw no point of another bus-ride to Panjim. Boredom was the last thing I expected I'd be fighting. Not having the constant push of having to get up for work everyday meant I really didn't have anything to aim for. Put more simply I just didn't have anything to do. So I forced upon myself a plan. Today: head North to the Vagator / Chapora area I'd read next to nothing about. Tomorrow: Old Goa. The day after that I was going home.

I started off at the 'Oxford Arcade' which was a convenience store next door to Anjuna Palms. I couldn't for the life of me think of a use for it, Goa was after all super-cheap to eat out in. As a result it always seemed completely dead, but again I had to remind myself that I would be home again well before things really started to pick up.

I still had the moped which was now becoming an extension of me as I casually kicked off the stand. I was now into flat, picturesque agricultural land with I'd noticed a lot more livestock present, including the usual cow stood motionless in the road. As I ground to a halt I found myself caught short and needing to head into the undergrowth for cover at the double, unceremoniously dumping the bike at the side of the road. As I relieved myself I noticed a small pond of water like an oasis in the baking heat, which begged to be investigated. Its residents were at first glance sickeningly slimy mutations writhing about in their cesspit. Closer inspection revealed the privileged sight of hippos in the wild, basking in their cooling bath, looking over at me suspiciously with disapproving glances. Another of the many special moments Goa had gifted me.

The fuel light flashed just as I happened upon a petrol station. As I pulled to a halt at the pump, another taste of the unexpected. I was ushered from the bike like royalty, the attendant removing the fuel cap for me and proceeding to fill her up. Once again, I told myself "this is India", where you were made to feel good even with a task as mundane as this.

Vagator was predictably underwhelming, the main attraction of its main strip seeming to be the 'Mango Tree' restaurant which I planned to visit for dinner. I arrived at a large car/coach park. which overlooked steep craggy, dangerous-looking cliffs down to a fairly inaccessible beach below. A crowd of youngsters were gathered toward the edge which I hoped would ignore me, but alas I found myself surrounded by them.

The conversation started off civil enough with the usual prodding of names/background, through to casual and then more aggressive sales technique regarding the usual bracelets or whatnot. Not only were Indians the best waiters in the world, they were also the best salesman. To have the sort of techniques they were using on me drummed into them at such an early age was frightening, but I guess for them the only way out of poverty. From there the conversation descended into mockery when they got the impression I wasn't buying. A young girl in particular pretending she could not understand me, "You Unglish?", "From NoCastle?" before miraculously figuring it all out to the rapturous approval of her peers "English!", "from Newcastle". I didn't get it, I didn't care, but things were now about to take a much more sinister turn. The oldest of the girls were barely in their teens, but wore the colorful dresses of their elders, with full makeup amateurishly applied. They continued with the incessant questioning, "What do you want?" as if I was actually there for something. "I don't want anything" raised concerned expressions."I'm just here for the view". With that, they played their final card. "Do you want a good time?". With that I stood up to leave in disgust. Part of me was sad that such a young girl needed to do this, but I didn't have a lot of sympathy for this particular gang. As I headed off ,a few more venomous, childish insults were thrown my way out of frustration, just as the heavens opened.

Behind the coach park was a wood of sorts that looked like decent shelter for now. As I stood under a tree I noticed a small bright orange hut with no obvious markings that nonetheless looked inviting, and on closer inspection revealed an opening. There were three people crammed inside a square area not a lot bigger than a bus-stop. As I approach they waved me in. "Come inside my friend". As I squeezed my large, ungainly frame in, a man was stood behind a wooden counter with his two friends the same side as myself. They were smoking cannabis of course but the man behind the counter's gaze had not left me. A tense moment passed before he asked "What would you like?". For a moment I froze, remembering the last conversation I had in the coach park, but looking past him I made out a fridge and the penny dropped. "Kingfisher please!". I actually found myself in the smallest, most primitive 'bar' I'd ever seen. But as the kingfisher (stubby) flowed (for the grand sum total of 20Rs) and the locals engaged me in Test match chat, I may as well have been in the Dog and Duck back home. Only here, there really weren't any, and I mean any, superfluous features, if any features at all.

As the sun steamed off the rain amongst the trees, I was waved off by the three guys after my second stubby, thinking that I'd just experienced the worst and best of Goa in less than fifteen minutes. Out of the undergrowth I noticed establishments geared for the high season's cool kids. Internet cafes, gaming rooms, bars, cafes and restaurants. All closed , lifeless and in disrepair. Back towards civilization was a bookshop, open, surprisingly. Not being a big reader myself I only managed a small glance around the neat but sparse shelves when the shopkeeper, an old, grey, friendly-looking man advertised that they also buy books. As it happened I still had a couple of books lying around back at Anjuna Palms so I promised him I'd bring them before I left for home. He seemed over the moon with that.

After what seemed like an age I was back in the saddle, and heading towards Chapora. What followed was undoubtedly the steepest hill I'd ever descended, and pretty scary on a moped with Indian traffic. At the bottom, in contrast to the stress and noise of the road was a tranquil stretch of coast, still and deserted, which begged you to stop and look out to the milky sea and mountains beyond. Other than that, there was nothing here of note or worth stopping to investigate.

After a horrendous moped hill climb, I confidently pulled up outside the Mango Tree and ordered a Kingfisher. The bar-stools were almost on the road and was a great spot to watch the world go by. I perched myself up, safe in the knowledge I was doing something not possible back home. Had health and safety gone too far? does it really improve our lives? Not from where I was sitting. The Mango Tree was a haven in the middle of, let's be honest, a pretty dead town, at least this time of year. There were a few ex-pats present, with the usual newspaper in hand. I couldn't imagine living here. I was bored in a day, but strangely time passed by quickly that day and before I knew it, it was getting dark.

Eventually I hauled myself up from the stool I'd gotten far too comfortable in, and investigated the main seating area, which was completely deserted. I took a seat at a table designed for at least six, yet still a waitress appeared immediately. Only one choice here, Chicken Biryani. This was a bit special though, as it came with a few side dishes that really hit it out the park, chief of which was an absolutely delicious Marsala sauce accompaniment, which was literally a pot of spicy joy that can't be justified with words. The pickles and the naan bread deserve a mention too. As I tucked in I felt sad that maybe I wouldn't taste food this good ever again, or at least not for a very long time,so I took my time and savoured it. I noticed a sign advertising a film about to start, so I settled in with a few more kingfishers to enjoy Troy.

The road back was pitch dark, and as I neared Anjuna Palms another site you don't see everyday. Cows, and lots of them, lying in the road asleep. These sacred animals of course can't be touched, you've got to go round them. Yes, even the buses.

Chapter 15 : Old Goa

My penultimate day in Goa began with the familiar melancholy of leaving something you love behind. I looked around my makeshift setup with the cold reality that this time tomorrow I'd be packing up and this would no longer be home, the desk in the corner reclaimed by my rodent friend as if I'd never been here at all. It was a feeling I didn't really want to shake, as it focused my mind to wring every last drop from the place, to appreciate and to enjoy.

I took the bus to Mapusa one last time, I'd even miss this most underwhelming of places I thought as I swan-necked the crowd looking for the stand to Old Goa. Time was passing too quickly, as, without delay, the connecting bus rolled into position. Like Vagator and Chapora the day before, I hadn't briefed myself at all about my destination, and as predictable as ever, I was in for a surprise.

The one nagging aspect of Goa which I couldn't get used to was the general shabbiness of the place. Most buildings were in a horrendous state of disrepair, some of them barely standing, roads were cracked and heavily potholed, with pavements being a rarity. It was an untidy, smelly, slapdash mess which really got to you at times, and made you crave the glass and chrome modernity of home. Old Goa, as it happens, was the exception to the rule.

As the coach neared its destination there were smooth roads, lined by well kept gardens. cool minimalism compared to the boiling pot of Calangute. This was a very religious place dominated by impressive churches and statues, none of which really fired my imagination. Maybe I'd been spoilt with the architecture back home. Regardless, I explored the first building, the enormous Basilica of Bom Jesus and was immediately thrown out for toting a camera. As it happens I lost most of my photos anyway, thanks to the demise of Bebo.

In an adjacent building, I happened upon a museum of all the usual artifacts you'd expect to see in a similar establishment the world over. One section though, was a protest against the commercialism of Calangute in a (mostly black and white) photographic gallery format. As I studied each picture in turn, a shiny new Subway (the sandwich franchise) with the slogan "Progress?" sticks in the memory, but many others showed the decimation of the original beautiful Calangute into collection of hotels, bars and restaurants it is today. I took a moment to pause. The overall impression I got was that, amongst the people at least, commercialism wasn't welcome, something imposed on them by a hated totalitarian government. But what about the boy in Coffee Day? or at the SeaRock? or at the Crumbland gig? they all seemed so optimistic about the future, they embraced it. One thing's for sure, as I left the museum I really wasn't sure if I was welcome here or not.

Just opposite,the ominous Sacred Heart of Jesus peered down at me, casting a calming shadow. It was a dull, overcast sort of day, made even more gloomy by his expression. Old Goa was a bastion of Christianity, and although the images I'd just seen didn't seem to represent those values I felt comforted that, here at least, we were all under one God.

Over the road by the tourist information and coach stop was a another attraction of sorts. I had time to kill so I ventured in to hurriedly catch the tail end of a group of tourists on some sort of light-hearted, guided tour on the history of Jesus himself. This was, in essence, a nativity play of corridors and tacky displays ,complete with inns, stables, wise-men etc etc, hilariously culminating in an image of the man himself dramatically beamed by projector onto the wall above us. To wide-eyed gasps from audience, I recognized the image as Robert Powell in his 1977 role as Jesus of Nazareth, sniggering under my breath. I don't think anyone else got the joke.

Chapter 16: Last Day in Goa

Time and reality had finally caught up with me and, after a month's 'sabbatical' in another continent, this was the final morning. The bed sheets that Felix's wife had kindly laundered for me never felt completely dry, but their methods were more primitive here, one last reminder that I hadn't really missed the mod-cons of back home at all. As I clambered to my feet my remaining pile of clothes, unceremoniously flung in the corner of the floor, were scooped up and dumped into my still-open case in one flowing movement. Amongst them, I only needed my clothes for today, and, it being a special occasion, the journey home too.

Documents were the next item on my task-list for today, which in turn were quickly dealt with by clearing out my only piece of furniture, the desk in the corner. As I meticulously sifted through the items to keep or to bin, I fondly recalled the incident with the rat way back on my arrival. With those sorted, I was struggling to find other things to do, so with the communal, makeshift, but surprisingly effective brush made from twigs, I gave the room a final once-over and made the bed. Looking around it was as though I was never here. I'd mainly kept my own company after all.

The intentionally long, lingering shower again focused my thoughts on our differing cultures. There was no hot water here, the wash-facilities were barely standing, and must've broken every self-imposed health and safety rule in the book back home. But, at the end of the day, it worked. Isn't that all that matters? Tomorrow, I'd have a whole set of irrelevant, unimportant concerns. Today I had none.

On the table outside I gathered up the remaining books that Roishin had left behind, and just as I'd promised to the book-keeper in Vagator a couple of days earlier, I caught the bus to his shop. The grey, wizardly looking gentleman greeted my with a beaming smile and open arms, like the return of his prodigal son. I was clasping a collection of books, (a couple of my travel guides and a sci-fi thriller), that, to me had no value at all. However, on clapping his eyes on them, the old man turned very serious and businesslike. In yet another unexpected turn of events, he rapidly offered me a surprisingly high price for the battered books I no longer had a use for. Looking around the bare but neat shelves I could see that he took a great pride in his shop, and I suppose in the same way a guitar-shop owner acquires a desirable second-hand instrument to display to his customers, he seemed to believe my books would enhance his shop window somewhat, so I gladly accepted his generous offer, which would be enough to make my last few hours a lot more comfortable than expected.

It was still morning as I arrived back at Anjuna Palms, with 3pm being departure time. I'd planned on a haircut and shave before I left, so, for one last time, I set off down the road to Baga or more specifically the village halfway. This was about as 'authentic Goa' as it got, a tiny, sign-less wooden shack, but as I sat myself down I was reminded again... Does that matter? Do we need anything more? I was slightly taken aback by the person staring back at me in the mirror. My hair had grown to shoulder-length and I was deeply tanned, but my cheek still hadn't fully healed up from my incident down the sewer.My stubble had grown more rapidly than usual, and for once didn't look like an adolescent's patchy efforts. Before my trip I built up my fitness and may have even looked on the gaunt side. I was stressed and hung up on life's worries with a terrible complexion to go with it. Now though I looked calm, relaxed and healthier,with clear skin and glint in my eye, opened up to the world. As the young lad cut away my locks, the new me disappeared, never to be seen again. I had one last task in Goa, my sandals had lasted the course, just, but now it was time to keep a promise I made.

Anjuna beach looked bleak today, lifeless and unwelcoming. As I approached the wall where I first met the impressive young boy, he was nowhere to be seen. As I put the sandals down on the flat concrete surface I half expected to be mobbed again or at least see children playing, but it was cold and silent, as if there wasn't a soul for miles. I wonder if he ever got his sandals I promised him?

One last time, I looked out onto the Arabian Sea. My time was almost up and soon everything I had looked forward to for the months leading up to this trip would become just another memory. After everything I'd done and everyone I'd met along the way, here I was again, alone on a beach, much like the way it began. Nevertheless, I raised a glass to them, in my imagination at least, as now it was time to go home.

Final Chapter : The Journey Home

It was now mid-afternoon in Anjuna. I trudged back to Anjuna Palms for the last time with great sadness, it had only seemed like yesterday when I first explored this place. The gang at the bike shop waved as usual, but as I announced my departure they dropped their usual sales pitch immediately, posing for a photograph. For the last month I'd passed them at least once every day, always with a friendly hello, some days they'd even been my only human contact, so as I and the ancient-looking man struck a pose I felt a connection breaking for good. Maybe he'd seen my type, the lone British traveler, lost in the world, a thousand times before. Maybe he understood me more than I'd ever know. He offered me his hand and a surprisingly firm handshake, along with a knowledgeable look that re-assured me it was time, no regrets.

Felix's whole family were waiting for me when I arrived back at the hostel. His wife had been like a mother to me at times, doing my laundry, advising me on the pitfalls of everyday Goa life and generally looking after me in general, always with a welcoming smile. Their two children had looked at me partly in fear, partly as some form of entertainment, but here they seemed generally sad to see me go, the young boy even showing me some of the moves he'd picked up whilst watching me train on the roof.

Felix, as ever, seemed detached, as he patiently waited for the formalities to cease. I took one last glance at the terrace, my adopted home, and pictured us all sat around the table, drinking and putting the world to rights from our perch like faded ghosts. A snapshot in time captured forever. Now though, everything had been cleared away, ready for the next round of hopefuls, ready for a brand new set of memories to be made. Goodbye Anjuna Palms.

I just about managed to squeeze myself into Felix's tiny box of a car, and we were on our way, the scenery passing by like a videotape in reverse. Munchies, the internet cafe over the road, the bike shop, and onto the leafy main strip. A mild panic took hold, I'd never see this place again would I? Felix was a man of few words, but, just as he did on arrival, he brought a calming focus to the situation "Did you enjoy your stay ?"

Of course I couldn't answer, I hadn't the words to do it justice.

After a mostly politely silent but relaxing journey, we again found ourselves back at Goa Airport. Felix, despite my protests, fulfilled his final duty of removing my case and guitar from the boot. As we stood shaking hands I looked upon him with some envy. Here was a man fully in control of his life, a fantastic family and his own business in an amazing part of the world, whereas I was returning back to the drizzle of North Shields to an empty house and a job I hated. True, he probably struggled to make ends meet, but he had something I didn't have, happiness. And right at that moment in time I would've gladly swapped places with him.

The departure lounge was small, but unlike most things in Goa, welcomingly modern and clean. My progress through security was completely unhindered until a smartly uniformed lady unceremoniously dumped my bottled products into a square plastic container for confiscation. There was no argument, no bureaucracy or further delay, simply a matter of I'd gone over the allowed limit, and with a polite smile I was moved along to the gate.

The plane itself was virtually empty, bar a few business types. Usually I fly economy class, the lowest of the low, crammed in with the commoners, but here I had all the space in the world, all three seats to myself and spaces all around. The air hostess was dressed in the same beige hues as the security attendant, and like most Goan ladies, absolutely immaculate. The lack of passengers made her job easier of course, but I've never known an air-stewardess to be more in control and responsive to everyone's requests.

As the beautiful landscape of Goa faded from view forever, the path ahead seemed gloomy, and a whole lot less colourful, so to distract myself I grabbed a publication tucked away in the seat in-front. The very first article was a commentary on the values of the West vs the

East. The struggle against capitalism and greed and of our forgotten human values and standards. If Goa had taught me one thing, its that we'd become detached from the things that really matter; joy, happiness, love and kindness, in favour of a constant push to selfishly further our careers and earn more money. I was reminded again of the picture display in Old Goa, but also, contrary to that, the young men I'd met wanting to better themselves, of essentially yearning to be more western. Who was right? India is a poor country, some would say a failing country, but on whose judgement? It certainly taught me a lot about my attitude towards life and others.

As night fell, I found myself once again in the international terminal of Mumbai airport, a place which didn't hold many fond memories. Out of self-protection I restricted my movements to a set of waiting chairs and settled in for a long night before my flight in the late hours. Here, I was safe from the parasites I'd encountered on arrival and I could just relax and people watch. As I gazed up at the flickering noticeboards and observed the general hectic activity, I could feel my eyes slowly beginning to close, still with thoughts of Goa buzzing around my head. It was as though I'd left its comforting bubble where time had stood still and now I was back in the real world like a newborn baby exposed to the cold air for the first time.

As I began to fade out of the room, a blob of pastel-shaded colour caught the corner of my eye. Now fully alert, a group of Geishas glided across the floor in front of me. Years of training had ironed out any imperfections in their movement as, to the casual eye, they seemed to float across the room with no leg or arm movements at all, as though suspended on a cushion of air. The group of eight were identical in height and appearance, moving as a synchronized whole like pristine, precious china dolls. They seemed to be super-imposed onto the backdrop of the murky rabble behind them. As I gazed in appreciation a tall thin man reminiscent of the guard on arrival stood directly in my line of sight and issued a simple question to all present. "Air France?"

A number of us, including myself acknowledged him, as that was our connecting flight back to Charles De Gaulle before home, and with that he directed us away, giving no explanation. I never did find out if the domestic terminal was closed on my arrival in Mumbai, but as the man proudly ushered us into a restaurant I could see this was the compensation. A few of the others questioned him on what all this was about. "Complementary" said the man. I sat down to enjoy my last meal in India. A buffet of sorts, watered down from incomparable Goan food, but still a fine feast, and one last, kind gesture from a nation I'd taken into my heart. I poured myself one last glass of Kingfisher and raised my own, personal, private toast.

As the gate opened, an animated English women, probably in her fifties, was brazenly pushing her luck with a collection of bottled alcohol and a colossal, but strangely skinhead ginger, armed guard, very similar to the guy back in Anjuna. He handled her like a true professional, calmly stating the law but also, despite his frightening size, connecting with her and even making her smile. He made her out to be the aggressor, the enemy of the peace as the crowd turned against her with sighs of disapproval. Again, this was the difference between us and them right here. I can only imagine a similar situation back home, a jobsworth, an escalation, delays mixed in with a good helping of frustration and bad blood. Here, none of that mattered. As a total anti-climax, my last action in Goa was to offload all of my remaining money at a ridiculously expensive excuse for a duty free, and so, cleared out with my newly acquired bottle of water in hand. I boarded the plane home.

Charles De Gaulle airport was more like a small city, with huge jumbos passing over bridges of an intricate internal road network. I was back in the cold modern, technological world. The comfortable departure lounge quenched my strange cravings I had back in Goa, all the chrome and glass I could handle and more. Something was missing though. The colour and smells were gone in place of clean air and grey. I was a number again, here to be processed, stamped and moved along the conveyor belt. Bright modern adverts for aspirational living once again clambered for my attention. For the first time in my life I could see the shallowness of it all, the meaningless daily pursuit of money and status by mobile toting suits with laptops. I suppose being in Goa had shown me more about humanity in a month than I'd seen for most of my adult life, but with each passing moment I was getting further away.

The call for the final leg back to Newcastle airport snapped me out of my private pity-party, as the very mention of my birthplace filled me with an unexpected but very familiar sense of pride. As we set off I recalled my darkest days in Goa, where I questioned myself and my motives. I was simply an Englishman returning from a holiday, nothing more. I couldn't have coped any longer in the place, boredom had kicked in, I'd seen it and done it., but the experience had still been "A lesson in Life".

In the years that followed I always wanted to put into words the events and experiences of my trip to Goa in August 2006 and, ten years later, I'm now about finish the story.

I really hope you enjoyed the journey.

Looking out over the horizon the sun was now blindingly high in the sky.

Next stop: Home.

19191266R00048

Printed in Poland
by Amazon Fulfillment
Poland Sp. z o.o., Wrocław